D0908278

THE STATES AND THE NATION SERIES, of which this volume is a part, is designed to assist the American people in a serious look at the ideals they have espoused and the experiences they have undergone in the history of the nation. The content of every volume represents the scholarship, experience, and opinions of its author. The costs of writing and editing were met mainly by grants from the National Endowment for the Humanities, a federal agency. The project was administered by the American Association for State and Local History, a nonprofit learned society, working with an Editorial Board of distinguished editors, authors, and historians, whose names are listed below.

Mississippi

A Bicentennial History

John Ray Skates

W. W. Norton & Company, Inc.
New York

American Association for State and Local History
Nashville

Author and publishers make grateful acknowledgment to the following for permission to quote from archival sources and previously published material.

Mississippi Historical Society, for permission to quote from "World War II as a Watershed in Mississippi History," by John Ray Skates, Jr., in *The Journal of Mississippi History* 37, no. 2 (May 1975): 135–141.

Mississippi Department of Archives and History, for permission to quote from the Wailes Papers.

Roy H. Ruby, for permission to quote from "The Presidential Election of 1944 in Mississippi: The Bolting Electors" (M.A. Thesis, Mississippi State University, 1966).

The Southern Historical Collection, University of North Carolina Library, Chapel Hill, N.C., for permission to quote from the Thomas H. Maddox Papers, #1753, and from the Quitman Family Papers, #616.

Mrs. Barker French and the Department of History, Duke University, Durham, N.C., for permission to quote from "American Beginnings in the Old Southwest: The Mississippi Phase," by William B. Hamilton (Ph.D. dissertation, Duke University, 1937).

Published and distributed by
W. W. Norton & Company, Inc.
500 Fifth Avenue
New York, New York 10036

Library of Congress Cataloguing-in-Publication Data

Skates, John Ray.
Mississippi, a Bicentennial history.

(The States and the Nation series)
Bibliography: p.
Includes index.
1. Mississippi—History. I. Title. II. Series.
F341.S65 976.2 78–25931
ISBN 0–393–05678–3

Printed in the United States of America

1 2 3 4 5 6 7 8 9 0

Contents

Illustrations

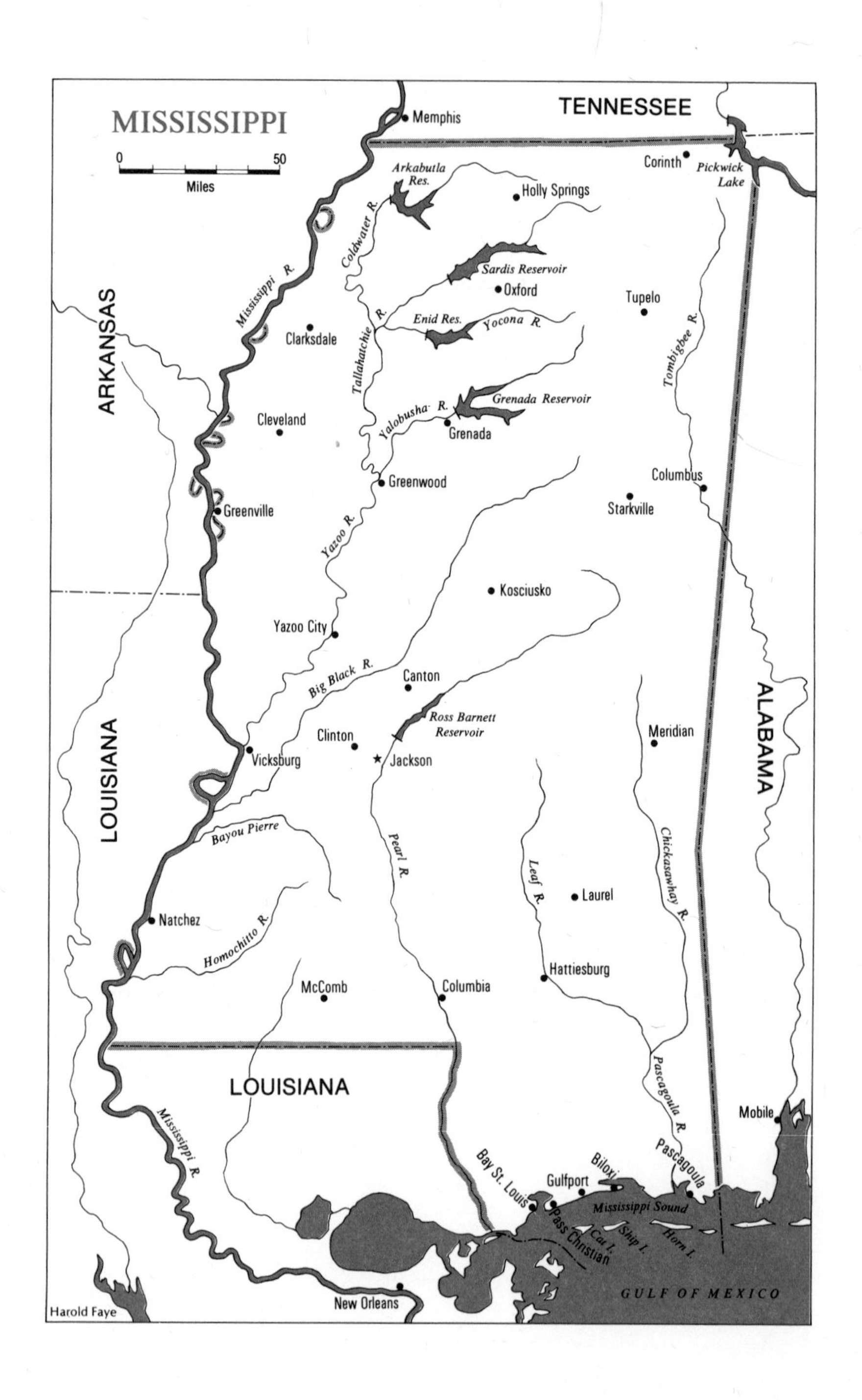
MISSISSIPPI
0
50
Miles
TENNESSEE
ARKANSAS
LOUISIANA
ALABAMA
LOUISIANA
Memphis
Corinth
Pickwick Lake
Arkabutla Res.
Holly Springs
Coldwater R.
Sardis Reservoir
Oxford
Tupelo
Mississippi R.
Tallahatchie R.
Enid Res.
Yocona R.
Clarksdale
Tombigbee R.
Grenada Reservoir
Yalobusha R.
Cleveland
Grenada
Greenwood
Columbus
Starkville
Greenville
Yazoo R.
Kosciusko
Yazoo City
Big Black R.
Canton
Ross Barnett Reservoir
Meridian
Clinton
Vicksburg
Jackson
Bayou Pierre
Pearl R.
Leaf R.
Chickasawhay R.
Laurel
Natchez
Homochitto R.
Hattiesburg
McComb
Columbia
Pascagoula R.
Mobile
Mississippi R.
Bay St. Louis
Gulfport
Biloxi
Pascagoula
Mississippi Sound
Pass Christian
Cat I.
Ship I.
Horn I.
GULF OF MEXICO
New Orleans
Harold Faye

Invitation to the Reader

IN 1807, former President John Adams argued that a complete history of the American Revolution could not be written until the history of change in each state was known, because the principles of the Revolution were as various as the states that went through it. Two hundred years after the Declaration of Independence, the American nation has spread over a continent and beyond. The states have grown in number from thirteen to fifty. And democratic principles have been interpreted differently in every one of them.

We therefore invite you to consider that the history of your state may have more to do with the bicentennial review of the American Revolution than does the story of Bunker Hill or Valley Forge. The Revolution has continued as Americans extended liberty and democracy over a vast territory. John Adams was right: the states are part of that story, and the story is incomplete without an account of their diversity.

The Declaration of Independence stressed life, liberty, and the pursuit of happiness; accordingly, it shattered the notion of holding new territories in the subordinate status of colonies. The Northwest Ordinance of 1787 set forth a procedure for new states to enter the Union on an equal footing with the old. The Federal Constitution shortly confirmed this novel means of building a nation out of equal states. The step-by-step process through which territories have achieved self-government and national representation is among the most important of the Founding Fathers' legacies.

The method of state-making reconciled the ancient conflict between liberty and empire, resulting in what Thomas Jefferson called an empire for liberty. The system has worked and remains unaltered, despite enormous changes that have taken place in the nation. The country's extent and variety now surpass anything the patriots of '76 could likely have imagined. The United States has changed from an agrarian republic into a highly industrial and urban democracy, from a fledgling nation into a major world power. As Oliver Wendell Holmes remarked in 1920, the creators of the nation could not have seen completely how it and its constitution and its states would develop. Any meaningful review in the bicentennial era must consider what the country has become, as well as what it was.

The new nation of equal states took as its motto *E Pluribus Unum*—"out of many, one." But just as many peoples have become Americans without complete loss of ethnic and cultural identities, so have the states retained differences of character. Some have been superficial, expressed in stereotyped images—big, boastful Texas, "sophisticated" New York, "hillbilly" Arkansas. Other differences have been more real, sometimes instructively, sometimes amusingly; democracy has embraced Huey Long's Louisiana, bilingual New Mexico, unicameral Nebraska, and a Texas that once taxed fortunetellers and spawned politicians called "Woodpecker Republicans" and "Skunk Democrats." Some differences have been profound, as when South Carolina secessionists led other states out of the Union in opposition to abolitionists in Massachusetts and Ohio. The result was a bitter Civil War.

The Revolution's first shots may have sounded in Lexington and Concord; but fights over what democracy should mean and who should have independence have erupted from Pennsylvania's Gettysburg to the "Bleeding Kansas" of John Brown, from the Alamo in Texas to the Indian battles at Montana's Little Bighorn. Utah Mormons have known the strain of isolation; Hawaiians at Pearl Harbor, the terror of attack; Georgians during Sherman's march, the sadness of defeat and devastation. Each state's experience differs instructively; each adds understanding to the whole.

The purpose of this series of books is to make that kind of understanding accessible, in a way that will last in value far beyond the bicentennial fireworks. The series offers a volume on every state, plus the District of Columbia—fifty-one, in all.

Each book contains, besides the text, a view of the state through eyes other than the author's—a "photographer's essay," in which a skilled photographer presents his own personal perceptions of the state's contemporary flavor.

We have asked authors not for comprehensive chronicles, nor for research monographs or new data for scholars. Bibliographies and footnotes are minimal. We have asked each author for a summing up—interpretive, sensitive, thoughtful, individual, even personal—of what seems significant about his or her state's history. What distinguishes it? What has mattered about it, to its own people and to the rest of the nation? What has it come to now?

To interpret the states in all their variety, we have sought a variety of backgrounds in authors themselves and have encouraged variety in the approaches they take. They have in common only these things: historical knowledge, writing skill, and strong personal feelings about a particular state. Each has wide latitude for the use of the short space. And if each succeeds, it will be by offering you, in your capacity as a *citizen* of a state *and* of a nation, stimulating insights to test against your own.

James Morton Smith
General Editor

Preface

Authors like Thomas Wolfe and William Faulkner often remarked on the ambivalence that native southerners feel for the South and its peculiarities. Contemporary Mississippians, perhaps more than other southerners, feel for their state a tension between love and frustration, fascination and rejection, for Mississippi was the last stronghold of the greatest American subculture, the South.

Thus, when I was discharged from the army in 1958 after two years in Germany, I was determined to return to my native Mississippi, pay my respects, and move somewhere else. Mississippi's image at that time was at a low ebb. The state already was attracting national attention for its stubborn opposition to the *Brown* decision that called for integrated public schools. In addition, only recently the sensational murder in Mississippi of black teen-ager Emmett Till had brought world attention. Largely through personal circumstances, I stayed, and as the years went by, I ceased to judge and condemn the people and characteristics of Mississippi and began trying to understand them. The best guide to the present being history, I began studying Mississippi's past. I soon found, too, that Mississippi could be a pleasant place to live. The weather is usually good, the people are generally courteous and friendly, and the needs of daily living are, generally speaking, easily and simply filled. It was in many respects an exciting, if often frustrating, place to live—exciting for a young man because change was in the air and frustrating because it seemed so slow in coming.

This book is not intended primarily as an encyclopedic history of Mississippi. In the first place, space limitations prohibited another cataloguing of the facts. In the second place, good general histories of Mississippi are already available. This volume is one explanation of those facts. The sponsors of this series asked for an interpretive essay—a personal summing up. Thus the facts contained in this book serve to illuminate and support an interpretive portrait of Mississippi. Few facts are included for their own sake. I will be pleased if my fellow historians find this volume interesting, but I have written it more for the general reader than for the expert in Mississippi history. Those who disagree with my interpretations of our state's history, will do so, I hope recognizing my good will for Mississippi, for I intend to live here for the rest of my days. Above all, please do not tell me to go back where I came from. I was born in Sharkey County and raised in Washington County. On both sides, my ancestors have lived in Mississippi for 150 years.

I wish to thank a number of people who aided, directly or indirectly, in the preparation of this book. The administration of the University of Southern Mississippi allowed me time away from my normal teaching duties. Without that consideration, I could not have completed the work in the short time available. The staff of the McCain Graduate Library at the University of Southern Mississippi, especially Claude E. Fike, University Archivist, and Henry Simmons, Director of the Mississippi Room, granted me space to work and their help in locating materials. Dr. John E. Gonzales, Professor of History at the University of Southern Mississippi, read the manuscript and offered advice. He, too, though a Louisianian, is addicted to Mississippi history. Miss Blannie Curtis, secretary for the Department of History, typed the manuscript in her usual quick and efficient manner. My wife, an English teacher for more than a decade, read the manuscript to save me from many grammatical embarrassments. Finally, I thank Mississippi State University's Dr. Glover Moore, who, seventeen years ago, took on the task of training an unpromising candidate to be a historian.

January 1978 JOHN RAY SKATES

Mississippi

Prologue

The Scene

THE air in summer is hot and wet, making one feel after a rain that he has just bathed in warm glue. The winter brings cold rains and crisp, cool days with air so clear and bright that one seems to move through crystal. To a New Englander, used to the rocky hills of Vermont or the boulder-strewn coast of Maine, the level sameness of the landscape would seem unimpressive. The westerner who measures other places by the grandeur of the Rocky Mountains would be equally unaffected. The highest point in Mississippi rises only to eight hundred feet, and the lowest lands lie at sea level, where the grassy coastal marshes merge with the Mississippi Sound. "To the west, along the Big River," wrote William Faulkner of his native state, once lay "the alluvial swamps threaded by black almost motionless bayous . . . impenetrable with cane and buckvine and cypress and ash and oak and gum." In the east are the highlands, red clay hills peopled first by the Choctaws and Chickasaws, who were, in their turn, elbowed out by the Scotch-Irish—a people as taciturn, proud, and insular as their old-world forebears. And in the south "the pine barrens and moss-hung liveoaks" give way to grassy marshes so flat and low and treeless that they seem "less of earth than water," [1] more a beginning of the sea than an end to the land.

1. William Faulkner, "Mississippi," in *Essays, Speeches and Public Letters by William Faulkner*, edited by James B. Meriwether (New York: Random House, 1965), p. 11.

William Faulkner spoke for many Mississippians when he wrote of his fascination with the land of Mississippi and the people that land molded and marked. "Home again, his native land; he was born of it and his bones will sleep in it," Faulkner wrote of his own feelings, "Loving all of it even while he had to hate some of it . . . he knows now that you don't love because: you love despite; not for the virtues, but despite the faults."[2]

Mississippians know, if many others do not, that Mississippi is a diverse land. Mississippians often grow frustrated at the tendency of post-World War II America to view Mississippi as a symbol or, worse still, as a geographic and social monolith—to see blacks only as oppressed toilers, planters as arrogant masters, and the rest as "rednecks," violent and ignorant. Or else romantics see the state and her people as a kind of *Gone With the Wind* set in Mississippi, an enlargement of aristocratic Natchez replete with fine horses, mansions, beautiful ladies, and handsome and hot-blooded gentlemen. To some black expatriates, Mississippi symbolizes inhumanity, unrelenting bitterness, and capricious violence. Like Sicily to the Italians, Mississippi has remained to Americans a world little understood. As in any stereotype, Americans have tended to find in Mississippi's past precisely what they set out to look for.

The influence of geography on the historical development of Mississippi weighs heavy, fostering sometimes subtle, oftentimes turbulent differences. In truth, Mississippi never has been a geographic or cultural monolith. The differing quality of the soil and topography in the state fostered from earliest times a sectionalism and a divergence of economic and political interests that lasted with varying intensity through 150 years. Generally, Mississippi's sectionalism has been an east-west cleavage over which was superimposed a loose and fluid planter-small farmer economic and political class separation. Situated in the lowlands, the prairies, and the river and creek beds of fertile soil, the planters pursued conservative politics and an agricultural system based first on slavery, then on sharecropping. The

2. Faulkner, "Mississippi," pp. 36, 42–43.

small farmers of the red-clay hills and the high country in the east had little use for slaves and fostered a political radicalism and egalitarianism reflected by Jacksonian politics before the Civil War and Populism afterwards. Even now, as sectional differences disappear, Mississippians with keen ears for speech patterns and pronunciation can tell not only where in the state the speaker comes from, but can guess with amazing precision the speaker's social origins.

For about thirty miles inland from the Gulf Coast, the soil is sandy, sterile, and produces only scrub oaks and small pines. Onto this coastal plain stepped d'Iberville and his French settlers in 1699, building their log palisade fort at Biloxi Bay. Like later Mississippians, these first Europeans learned that this coastal region would never prosper from its soil, and they moved on, first to Mobile Bay, then to New Orleans. The Gulf Coast today is alive with tourists and industrial growth, but these are largely phenomena of the last four decades. Until recent times, the coastal plain was a sparsely settled outpost of French, Spanish, and Catholic influences culturally linked more closely to New Orleans and south Louisiana than to north Mississippi.

North of the coastal plain from the Pearl River on the west to the Alabama state line on the east, the terrain becomes rolling, and the pine trees grow taller. In these piney woods, the topsoil is thin and infertile. Here no more than on the coast could cotton planters prosper. Until the timber boom of the late nineteenth century, these pine barrens supported only a sparse population. The piney-woods farmers eked a livelihood from herding livestock and planting subsistence crops in the bottom lands near streams. Egalitarian, independent, and poor even by Mississippi standards, the piney-woods people desired most of all to be left alone. With little interest in cotton and none in slavery, Civil War deserters and draft dodgers in this region challenged alike Confederate and Union attempts to impress them into the war. W. H. Sparks, a nineteenth-century traveler, observed that the piney-woods people sought an "open, poor, pine country which forbade a numerous population." Here they raised "immense herds of cattle, which subsisted exclusively upon the coarse grass and reeds which grew abundantly among the tall long-leafed pine.'' They were, according to Sparks, ''careless of the comforts of a better reared, better educated, and more intelligent people''; but through stock-minding, hunting, and growing a few vegetables, they ''in blissful ignorance enjoyed life after the manner they loved.''[3]

Mississippi's geographic and cultural heart lies in the red-clay and bluff hills that fan out from central Mississippi northward to the Tennessee line. Here is a microcosm of Mississippi—rich bottom lands along the rivers and creeks and thin, less fertile soil on the hillsides. Planters and slaves carved plantations from the bottoms, while the more numerous small farmers struggled to cultivate the red (and later gullied) soil of the hillsides. These hills are the Yoknapatawpha world of William Faulkner—arrogant planters, small-town merchants, enduring blacks, and tragic Indians.

In the northeast corner of Mississippi rise the highest hills in the state. These northeastern hills form the southern and westernmost foothills of the Appalachian Mountains, and they were home mostly to nonslaveowning, independent, small farmers, culturally, politically, and economically more akin to their highland cousins in East Tennessee than to their fellow slaveowning, cotton-planting Mississippians in the south and west. The counties of these hills have always counted the lowest proportion in the state of blacks in their population. In the 1970 census, Alcorn, Itawamba, and Tishomingo reported a black population respectively of only 11.7, 4.6, and 4.4 percent. Yet the hillsmen did share other characteristics of their fellows—poverty, an independent, small-farmer agrarianism, and a Scotch-Irish insularity.

To the east, running along the western bank of the Tombigbee river in a rolling, productive, thirty-mile-wide arc, is the prairie. This open country forms an arm of the black belt, that great cotton kingdom of the Old South that stretches across south-central Alabama. Until after World War II, the prairie was a land of cotton, where planters and farmers sought to emu-

3. W. H. Sparks, *The Memories of Fifty Years* (Philadelphia: Claxton, Remsen and Haffelfinger, 1870), pp. 331–332.

late the Natchez barons but failed to reach their heights of wealth or pretentiousness. By the 1970s the soil was mostly given over to the raising of livestock.

Perhaps the most unusual soil region in Mississippi lies as flat as a tabletop over the northwestern quarter of the state. The Yazoo-Mississippi Delta is, in fact, only a part of the lower Mississippi River valley flood plain, and it is little different from adjacent areas across the river in Arkansas and Louisiana. (The barons who lived on the Natchez bluffs had many of their land holdings in the flat, fertile lands across the river in Louisiana.) Yet the Delta has played an uncommon role in Mississippi history. Because of flood problems, the Delta was extensively settled only after the Civil War. As the early settlers built levees to hold back the water, the region developed into a plantation society, not of the Old South, but of the new. Delta settlers who drained the lands, built the levees, and cleared the forests achieved some of the grandiose style of their prewar Natchez counterparts. Here the plantation system still dominates, in recent times with machines and chemicals rather than sharecroppers. The planters still grow and curse cotton, though cattle and soybeans have achieved growing prominence since World War II.

To the non-Mississippian, indeed to many natives, the diversity of Mississippi's countryside and her people would perhaps go unnoticed except for the most dramatic and sudden changes in surroundings. Even the uninitiated must feel the sky pressing down as he suddenly drops from the bluff hills into the Yazoo-Mississippi Delta. The diversity is there, and, subtly, geography has molded the people. Although white Mississippians have been forced since 1954 into an unusual unity by the civil-rights movement, the old distinctions, more delicate now, still persist. Occasionally still, the hill farmer sneers at the Delta planter. North Mississippi Baptists and Methodists condemn the sinful, loose, Latin ways of the Gulf Coast. Geography dictates demography, for despite the great exodus of Mississippi blacks to the ghettos of Chicago and Detroit, black Mississippians still live most numerously in those areas where their ancestors worked as slaves on cotton lands more than a century ago.

Such economic, political, and cultural diversity as Mississippi's geography has inspired has frequently been disguised, however, by the appearance of a high level of white unity, unity that has proven especially strong in times of racial stress. In the 1850s, during Reconstruction, and after the Supreme Court's desegregation decision in 1954, fears among whites of losing control of the racial *status quo* overrode normal sectional and economic differences. In such times an outsider, listening to a conversation among native white Mississippians, might conclude that the talkers are not citizens of a state so much as members of a club, if not all members of the same family.

To the outsider, white Mississippians' clanlike insularity and defensiveness is the most difficult characteristic to understand. Marked at its worst by a stubborn pride and at best by courageous independence, Mississippi's white men often instinctively believed that the affairs of their state were theirs and theirs alone. So tribal were Mississippi whites when defending the racial *status quo* that they sometimes failed to distinguish between public affairs and private matters. When James Meredith entered Ole Miss in 1962, white Mississippians perceived him not as a citizen exercising his rights, so much as an uninvited guest crashing a garden party.

The insularity and independence of Mississippi whites is rooted deep in history. Much of what is now Mississippi passed in the eighteenth century successively through the hands of the French, the British, and the Spanish. Yet, long before the area passed to the United States in 1798, the land already was peopled by Anglo-Americans. As the population increased before the Civil War, Mississippi grew mainly from immigration out of the states of the older South. In the thirty years before the war, North Carolina furnished more new Mississippians than any other state, followed by South Carolina, Tennessee, Georgia, and Virginia. Few foreign immigrants or northerners or New Englanders leavened this mass of Southern Scotch-Irish Methodists and Baptists.

They came from the Southern Piedmont, and when they arrived, they became farmers, not planters. Pushing the Choctaw and Chickasaw Indians aside, they rapidly filled up the state.

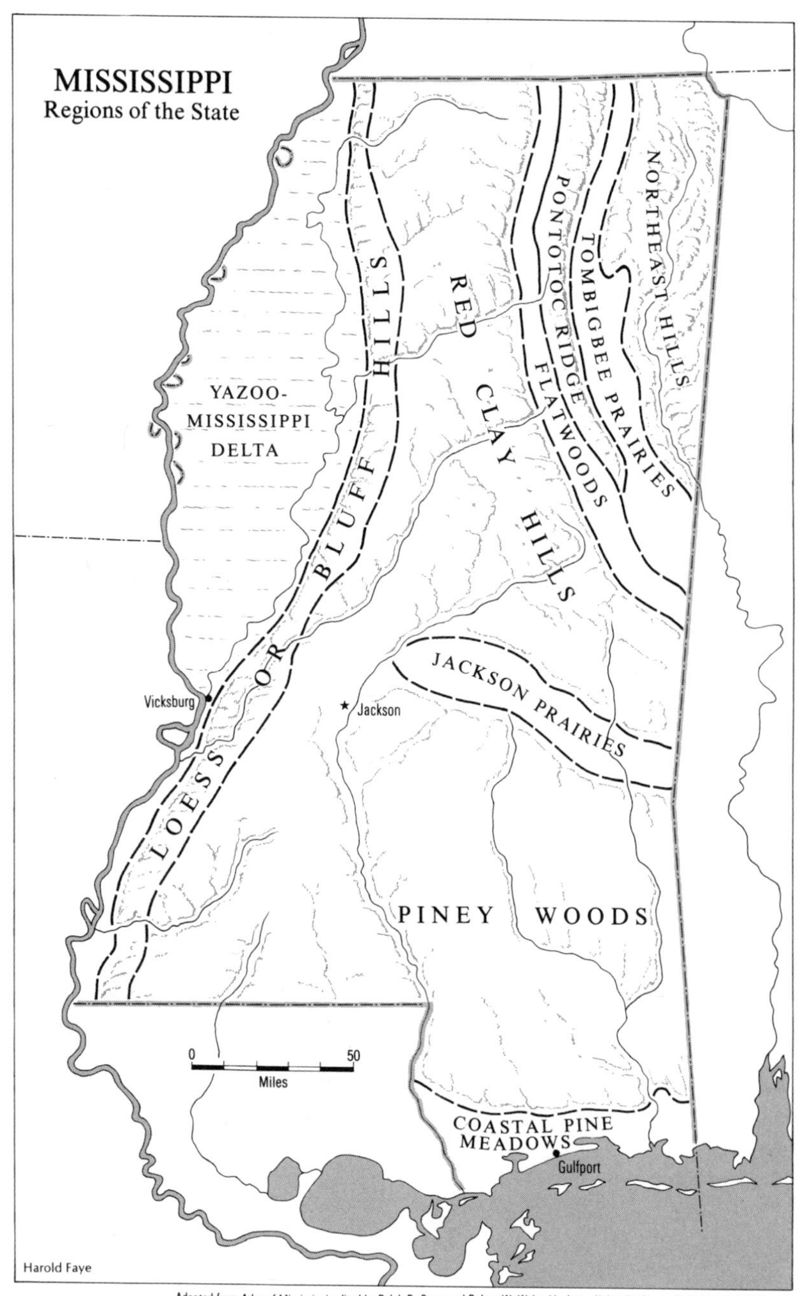

Adapted from *Atlas of Mississippi*, edited by Ralph D. Cross and Robert W. Wales (Jackson: University Press of Mississippi, 1974), p.6

More than 97 percent rural by the time of the Civil War, nearly all Mississippians earned their livelihood from the soil. With the exception of Natchez in the southwest and later the Delta, Mississippi became and remained a land mostly of small farmers.

Being backwoods yeomen, Mississippians early developed a frontier egalitarianism, a democracy with a little "*d*," which persists to this day. The tenets of Jacksonian faith—independence, political equality, supremacy of the legislative branch, suspicion of wealth, distrust of refinement and sophistication, and a hostility toward intellectual abstraction—all distinguish the white Mississippian. Set race aside, and he is among the most democratic of Americans.

Maybe more than most Americans, he has been marked by the forces of history. He knew that progress was not inevitable, nor was victory in war always assured. Compelled by his heritage to guard the racial *status quo* first in a disastrous defense of slavery, then a century later in an equally unsuccessful resistance to desegregation, and in the interim largely ignored by the dominant sections of the nation, the white Mississippian developed a sense of isolation, a parochialism bordering sometimes on paranoia, unfamiliar to most Americans. A lack of mobility aggravated this insularity. After the large migrations of the antebellum years, few came; according to the census of 1900, only 14 percent of Mississippians were born outside the state. The figure remained precisely the same in 1970. Cast in the role of racial scapegoat in a nation proud of its righteousness and poverty-stricken in a nation of plenty, the white Mississippian drew in upon himself, reacted sometimes by attempting to make badges of honor of his peculiarities and shortcomings. If he felt misunderstood, it is perhaps because, at times, he was.

Caught up with the whites, sometimes in good will, often as pawns, always as mudsills, were the blacks—until recently aliens in their own land. Slavery was introduced into Mississippi by the French in the eighteenth century. Until the 1830s limited mainly to the Natchez area, the slave population grew in that decade faster than the number of whites. Like their masters, they too came from the states of the older South and by the Civil War outnumbered the whites nearly six to four. Freed by the war, blacks saw their lot improve only slightly. They knew a poverty more degrading than that of their white neighbors. Materially hardly better off than as slaves, they were, like their white counterparts, some of America's forgotten people. Given the opportunity to escape to the industrial cities of the North following World Wars I and II, the Negro belied the white man's myth of black contentment by leaving the state in unprecedented numbers. The black-white ratio in Mississippi, which stood in 1900 at six blacks to four whites, by 1970 had more than reversed in the population with 37 percent black to 63 percent white.

Treated with paternalistic patronage by upper-class whites or sadistic brutality by the lower classes, the black Mississippian was hardly more than a victim—his economic, social, and political status defined by the dominant white minority. Amazingly, he preserved and enlarged a black culture, strongly expressed in his music—the blues—his religious life, and in a vividly colorful speech, even while living in a society where whites dominated. Physical closeness and a certain economic interdependence between the races veneered a cultural and emotional chasm. Only as the twentieth century moves to a close have Mississippians, black and white, albeit with considerable prodding, begun to free themselves of the political, economic, and psychological bondage of race.

For a time in the history of Mississippi a third ethnic influence came from Indians. A strong force until the early nineteenth century, they were eventually overwhelmed. Their fate, if not unusual in American history, was tragic. When Hernando de Soto wandered aimlessly across Mississippi in 1541, perhaps thirty thousand Indians lived in the area that, 276 years later, was to become the state of Mississippi. By 1970, fewer than forty-five hundred remained. Twenty thousand Choctaws inhabited lands in the central and southeastern portions of the state. Forty-five hundred Chickasaws, culturally kin to the Choctaws, controlled the extreme north and spilled over into present-day Tennessee. The Natchez, equal in number to the Chickasaws, lived in the southwest, their principal settlement located near the town that today bears their name.

Contacts with European civilization eventually doomed Indian culture. Superior European technology destined the Indians' old pastoral existence for extinction, and later the American frontiersman's greed for new land left the Indians only two alternatives. They could give up their ancestral lands in Mississippi and move west, or they could face obliteration. The Natchez Indians were exterminated in a war with the French in 1729. Ironically for the remaining Mississippi Indians, the more they adapted to American ways, the more the backwoodsmen pressured them to give up their lands. Ultimately, what the Mississippi frontiersman wanted was not that the Indian adapt or assimilate, but that he cede his lands to the federal government, thereby creating a vast new public domain that settlers and speculators could then buy up at bargain rates. After statehood in 1817, that pressure became coercion. In three great cessions—Doaks's Stand in 1820, Dancing Rabbit Creek in 1830, and Pontotoc in 1832—the Choctaws and Chickasaws gave up all their remaining lands in Mississippi to begin a trek into Indian Territory in the West. All that reminds us that the land once was theirs are four thousand Choctaws still living in Neshoba, Winston, Leake, and Newton counties and the countless musical Indian names applied to rivers, creeks, towns, and counties.

There are a few other small ethnic groups. A small colony of Chinese, now numbering fewer than one thousand, lives in the Mississippi Delta. Italian families provide another cultural strain. Brought to the Delta in the late nineteenth century when the planters sought some alternative to black sharecroppers, these Delta Chinese and Italians produced descendants who soon became merchants and landowners themselves and provided an out-of-the-ordinary cosmopolitanism in an area where one would expect to find only planters and black tenants. On the Gulf Coast, descendants of French and Spanish settlers and a sizable Slavic community refute the prevailing notion of utter black-white uniformity. Yet, in the main, black and white Mississippians have lived through their history in a land with few other ethnic forces to soften the edges or cushion the impact between the two.

So the land was the field upon which Mississippians produced their history, and as the battlefield influences the battle, the history of Mississippi's people has been shaped by the land. Yet, for Mississippians and non-Mississippians alike, the meaning of that history is unclear, for Mississippi history often conjures images more than meaning, snapshots in time more than photographic essays. To some, the image is a fiery cross and a bullet-riddled black chained to a tree. Others see a snow-white cotton field dotted with stooping, singing blacks picking under the serious but benevolent gaze of the planter. To still others, Governor Ross Barnett appears in a news photo. He politely confronts James Meredith with an ordinance of interposition and as Meredith, the only black amid a phalanx of white United States marshals, attempts to enter the state office building, asks "Now, which of you is James Meredith?" To others, Mississippi means Natchez—great white-columned mansions so grand that the planters who built them were afflicted either with the worst case in American history of "keeping up with the Joneses" or with egos that made them think they were a new nobility. To some, the scene is Vicksburg in the Civil War, "The Gibraltar of the Confederacy." Against that backdrop is set a stubborn, tattered, proud, beaten yet defiant Confederate soldier forced to yield to overwhelming numbers after a gallant struggle. To others, the heroic Mississippian is a black—Medgar Evers, shot in the back in his own driveway and martyred to the cause of his people.

Those who look past the immediate image face a still more difficult problem in understanding Mississippi's past; for it lies warped and obscured, veiled by a tangled set of myths and symbols. For the native, the desire to turn to historical myths to explain the state's past, especially since the Civil War, has proved irresistible. The desire of other Americans to see Mississippi as a symbol became equally enticing. Before World War II, when Americans deigned to notice the state, it was as a symbol of poverty, ignorance, and cultural backwardness. After World War II, the civil-rights movement thrust Mississippi to national notice as a symbol of the worst of the South, a grotesque relic of racism, poverty, ruralism, and violence. In short, Mississippi's past has been stereotyped, if not caricatured, its historical currents never fully understood even by Mississippians. In the minds of some uninformed modern liberal puritans, the state is a symbol of the darkest forces in American history. In the view of the unreconstructed romantics, it is a dreamy, contented land filled with Uncle Remuses, devoted mammies, and a white gentry.

One of Mississippi's most cherished myths teaches that the state's history is replete with great leaders and notable men. Ask a native to identify the greatest historical figure from Mississippi, and he would name Jefferson Davis or L. Q. C. Lamar or Theodore Bilbo or Medgar Evers. Ask a Frenchman or a German or a New Yorker to name the greatest Mississippian, and his answer almost certainly would be William Faulkner. Therein lies an irony, for Mississippi's political leadership over the generations has been rather ordinary—especially in times of crisis, while her greatest legacy, unknown to most Mississippians, has been literary. Mississippians, more than others, have been true democrats—Jacksonians who believed that the commonest man could be plopped down in the governor's chair or a legislative seat and do the job. That belief is *true* democracy. Unfortunately, that process has not often produced leaders, and in times of crisis—secession in 1861, Ole Miss in 1962—it has produced men who either tried merely to find the crowd and get in front of it or who allowed themselves to be manipulated by stronger personalities.

Another myth that has furnished great solace to Mississippians, especially the post-Civil War genteel poor, is the moonlight-and-magnolia tradition—the pervasive idea that Mississippi before the war was a land of gracious plantations, peopled with contented darkies, refined gentlemen, and beautiful ladies, that white Mississippians are all descended from dashing Confederate colonels. In fact, Mississippi at the time of the Civil War was still a frontier. Mississippi as a cotton-slave state was, in 1860, less than a generation old. So the onset of the war slammed down a developing frontier; it did not lay waste a mature, noble, and culturally refined society.

Perhaps the myth that has furnished the most fuel for politicians and shaped the views of white Mississippians toward blacks, toward the federal government, and toward themselves is the set of persistent images surrounding the era of Reconstruction. Perceptions of Reconstruction molded the views of Mississippians for generations. First, Reconstruction furnished at least two generations of Mississippians with a convenient rationale for the state's lack of development. It was easy to say that Mississippi remained poor and unrevived because through misrule and corruption the Yankees had exploited and held back the state. Supposed black incompetence and alien carpetbagger rule, moreover, served as a justification and explanation for Mississippi's most noticeable modern characteristics—a sense of persecution and alienation from the rest of America and the determination of whites to deny black Mississippians any economic or political role except that of serf. Painting Reconstruction as a dark, dismal period of alien rule also served the Mississippi Democratic party well. For decades, Democratic politicians covered their lack of programs by the southern counterpart of "waving the bloody shirt." In the elections of 1963, for the first time since Reconstruction, the Republican party in Mississippi mounted a real campaign for the governorship, running Reubel Phillips against then Lieutenant Governor Paul Johnson, Jr. By 1963 the Mississippi Republicans were all white, as segregationist as the Democrats and economically more conservative. Yet, from his campaign, one would have thought that Johnson was running against the carpetbagger Adelbert Ames or at least the scalawag James L. Alcorn from the days of Reconstruction. Johnson painted lurid pictures of Negro rule, fiscal corruption, and federal intervention should the Republicans succeed. Johnson failed to mention that it was a fellow Democrat in the White House who ordered troops to Oxford to assure the admission of James Meredith and that by 1963 hardly a black belonged to the Mississippi Republican party. Nearly a hundred years after the fact, Reconstruction still had its political uses.

Reconstruction also furnished a powerful justification in the minds of white Mississippians for keeping blacks politically powerless. Whenever faced with the possibility of black political activism, white Mississippians justified the continued political suppression by pointing to the corruption, illiteracy, and incompetence of "Negro rule" during Reconstruction. What Reconstruction did in Mississippi was little; what later generations of Mississippians *thought* it did formed a powerful force in the Mississippi mind.

A theme that runs through the history of southern race relations is "the Negro is content with his situation." This too was a convenient myth to salve the consciences of whites and to justify segregation to outsiders; hence Mississippians throughout Reconstruction and the modern civil-rights movement blamed any efforts to upset the racial *status quo* on "outside agitators"—during the first Reconstruction, on the carpetbaggers; during the second, on the civil-rights workers and agents of the Justice Department. Of course Mississippi blacks on two occasions proved that they were anything but content with their lot. The slaves voted for change by running away from their plantations on the approach of the first Union army. Hundreds of thousands of their descendants refuted the myth of contentment by migrating to the industrial cities of the North.

A corollary to the myth of contentment is the idea that "Southern whites understand the black man best," or "leave us alone to deal with the race problem as we see fit." One need only read Richard Wright or, more recently, Ann Moody's *Coming of Age in Mississippi* to realize that a psychological chasm separated whites and blacks. As both authors point out, one of the hardest pressures to live with was the capricious and gratuitous violence that accompanied being black in Mississippi. Nor did physical proximity always produce understanding, for Richard Wright's first contacts with white Mississippians did not come until his teens. Both Wright and Moody equated their blackness with poverty. Because both were strong, neither was without hope and ambition; yet through the writings of both runs the theme that hopelessness and fatalism were a large part of the black condition. Finally, through the works of both authors runs the clear implication that much of the world of Mississippi blacks was hidden from whites.

The historian who successfully negotiates the mine field of myths in Mississippi history immediately finds himself confronted with paradoxes—double-edged historical legacies that puzzle the outsider and produce among Mississippians a strange ability to weld together illusion and reality. Perhaps anomalies are not uncommon in human history, but the eccentricities of Mississippi history pile atop one another—white and black, wealth and poverty, paranoia and pride, egalitarianism and racism, individualism and forced white unity, radicalism and reaction, honor and chicanery, political sterility and cultural fertility. A state that produced in a single generation Theodore Bilbo and William Faulkner cannot be unaware of historical irony.

Mississippi's history, perhaps because of the interlaced myths, paradoxes and ironies that fill the years, remains strangely uninterpreted. The facts have been recorded, yet no synthesis, aside from the traditional antebellum-postbellum, Old South-New South chronology and the white man-black man dichotomy, holds the eras together. More important, little attempt to relate the history of Mississippi to the broader history of the nation has yet been made.

The history of Mississippi may conveniently be divided into three eras—each with its own institutions, values, and characteristics. In the relationships of these chronological eras to the institutions, ideals, and values of the greater nation, one may see not only the eccentricities and uniqueness of Mississippi and her people, but also the effort of the state to fulfill American ideals. At various times Mississippians found themselves at odds with the nation. At other times their ideals and goals were little different from those of the nation as a whole.

Explored by the Spanish in the sixteenth century, settled by the French in the eighteenth, and passed successively thereafter from British to Spanish to American control, Mississippi by the late eighteenth century already was a part of the greater American frontier. She remained so until the decade of the 1830s. During the provincial and territorial years and even into the first two decades of statehood, the aspirations and institutions of Mississippi's people differed little from those of frontiersmen elsewhere. Driven by an ambition and individualism that modern Americans can hardly understand, Mississippians went to the wilderness for the land. Their houses were rude, and so were their institutions. Government was rudimentary, violence and chicanery common, and the values of independence, egalitarianism, and pragmatism much admired. Even before the creation of the Mississippi Territory in 1798, Mississippians viewed themselves as Americans, loyal to the national government. They saw themselves not as "southerners," a term which a short time later carried connotations of something other than complete Americanism, but as "westerners." After all, most Mississippians had been born in the seaboard states. Nor in that day did slavery seem peculiarly un-American. Slaves were not as numerous then in Mississippi as they would later become, nor were the white planters wedded to slavery irrevocably and psychologically as they later would be. Those other distinguishing peculiarities that later divided Mississippians from America—cotton culture, intellectual insularity, emotional defensiveness, and a myth-ridden history—were not yet apparent.

The most important ten years in Mississippi history came in the 1830s. In that decade, Mississippians for a variety of reasons embraced new institutions, values, and ideals that set the state at odds with American values, that changed the course of Mississippi history, making it diverge from mainstream America.

That dramatic divergence was set in motion when the Choctaw and Chickasaw Indians ceded the northern two-thirds of Mississippi, and the new lands were opened to settlement. Between 1820 and 1832 these two great tribes handed over to the United States government twenty million acres. There followed in the 1830s a rush of settlement and a hectic growth unparalleled in the state's history. The effects were immediate. Population in that single decade increased 175 percent. Land sold for $1.25 an acre, setting off a speculative boom, wildcat banking, easy credit, and "flush times," which came crashing down in the Panic of 1837.

The boom produced long-range effects even more important. Old institutions like cotton agriculture and slavery, hitherto limited to the southwest around Natchez, suddenly swept over the state. Cotton production soared, and that worshipped and cursed commodity was raised to an economic throne not to be pulled down for more than a hundred years. Slavery, an institution long established around Natchez, burst into the northern counties. The slave population increased in the 1830s by 197 percent, resulting in a ratio of 52 percent slaves to 48 percent whites by the end of that decade. Viewed previously as a necessary evil by some leading Mississippi politicians and planters, slaves now became more numerous and more profitable, and Mississippians changed their views to suit the new circumstances. By 1840 it was no longer possible to challenge slavery either as an economic system or as a system of social control. White supremacy not only was strengthened but became for most white Mississippians the only acceptable rationalization for slavery. Jacksonian frontiersmen flocked to the new counties and captured control for Democratic politics in the spirit of white egalitarianism. A rural, agrarian society developed, and the already waning power of the Natchez planters was overwhelmed. Mississippi developed a set of peculiar institutions with values, customs, and an economic system increasingly set apart from the rest of urbanizing, industrializing America. The events of the century that followed the 1830s would harden those institutions and make the state, by national standards, even more peculiar. Surely, Mississippi shared her new characteristics with her southern neighbors, but the changes in Mississippi proved deeper; Mississippians held to them longer and gave them up more reluctantly than any other southern state.

The Civil War and Reconstruction are credited with working a veritable revolution in the South. Obviously the slaves were freed, and Mississippians, excepting the 28,000 who died in the war, were economically leveled. To most historians, the era from 1861 to 1876 formed a watershed. It was, in fact, only an interval, for the same patterns that had come to dominate Mississippi in the 1830s—cotton, slavery, a rural agrarianism, high proportion of blacks to whites—re-emerged after the war. Cotton, if anything, strengthened its hold on Mississippians from 1865 to 1945. The rigid controls over the large black population formerly provided by slavery reappeared after Reconstruction in Jim Crow laws and customs. Sharecropping replaced slavery. Though after World War I blacks began migrating northward, the prewar preponderance of blacks in the population changed little. Mississippians remained poor, rural, and racially divided. Little changed except the names.

Neither did the agrarian revolt of the late nineteenth century, nor progressive agrarian reformers like James K. Vardaman and Theodore Bilbo in the eartly twentieth century, nor FDR and his New Deal fundamentally alter old patterns of thought and ways of behaving. Mississippi's people, both blacks and whites, in 1940 lived much as their ancestors had in 1840. Chained to cotton and white supremacy, living in greater poverty than a hundred years before, they felt isolated, ignored, misunderstood, and persecuted. Through the Civil War and Reconstruction, populism, progressivism, and the Great Depression, continuity and not change has been the hallmark of Mississippi history.

The Second World War began to break those institutional chains that bound Mississippians to their past. After 1945 virtually every peculiarity that had marked the state since 1840 was challenged and broken. King Cotton fell. Only in the Delta did he still presume to power following World War II, and even there he shared his throne with livestock and soybeans. While the belief in white supremacy that buttressed Jim Crow lingers in some minds, the formal, legal, and much of the customary proscription of blacks is now a thing of the past. The sharecropper is a relic, displaced by machines and chemicals. Mississippi moved to town with a population in 1970 that was 45 percent urban. The racial ratio, which stood only 75 years ago at 60 percent black to 40 percent white, has more than reversed, and the intensity of the race question abates accordingly. Only about 20 percent of Mississippians now derive their livelihood from the land, and far more wages are made from factories than from farms. Mississippians tasted affluence for the first time in World War II, and they liked it. No sharecropper, working in a Pascagoula shipyard for more money in a week than he ever saw before in a year, would return to north Mississippi to walk behind a mule.

Mississippi, then, is both a land of divisions and of unity—split internally by geography and race. Yet racial considerations forced on white Mississippians a false unity that often overrode sectional and economic cleavages. Persistent insularity and suspicion of the outside—characteristics fostered by poverty and the necessity among whites to defend first slavery and then Jim Crow—produced a myth-encrusted history filled with paradoxes, ironies, and anomalies that proved crippling to Mississippians and baffling to others. One must step back from those myths and move away from the old ways of viewing Mississippi history and view it afresh. Perhaps it is time to abandon the old chronological chasm that divides antebellum from postbellum and look instead at a Mississippi history divided into three periods. Likewise, perhaps the day has come when one may frankly admit that at least for the longest of those periods, from the early nineteenth century down into our own time, continuity, not change, has characterized Mississippi's past.

1

Spain, France, and the Colonial Frontier

AMERICANS traditionally look for their heritage in the British Colonies, which by the early eighteenth century stretched along the Atlantic Coast from New England to Georgia. Yet many states owe their beginnings to other great colonial powers of sixteenth- and seventeenth-century Europe. Mississippi's origins lie in the military and commercial designs of Spain and France. Spain first explored this wilderness, and France first settled it. Mississippi's colonial frontier is as much the story of French voyageurs, fur trappers, and Indian traders, as of British farmers. Mississippi's pilgrims spoke French, paddled canoes, and said mass.

The lower Mississippi River valley had been explored and claimed for France by Robert Cavelier, Sieur de La Salle, in 1682. La Salle had followed up his claim by leading an ill-fated and unsuccessful attempt in 1685 to settle on the Gulf Coast. Lost on the Texas coast, the settlement fell prey to Indians, and La Salle himself was eventually murdered by mutineers. Yet French plans for a colony in "Louisiana" did not die with La Salle.

In December 1697 the Sieur de Remonville, prominent friend of La Salle, addressed a memoir to the Count de Pontchartrain, Louis XIV's Minister of Marine, on the "importance of establishing a colony in Louisiana.'' Remonville extolled the richness of the lower Mississippi River Valley.

> The country abounds in everything necessary for the convenience of life. It produces two crops of maize, or Indian corn annually. It is an excellent article of food; and, when one becomes accustomed to it, the corn of Europe can be easily dispensed with. There are also a great variety of grapes, which make excellent wines. . . . The country is beautifully diversified with hill and dale; the air is pure and invigorating and the winter is seldom felt there.[1]

He went on to promise great profit from the fur trade, from abundant iron, lead, tin, and copper deposits, timber for ship building, and fine woods "for ornamental work, no less beautiful than the Brazilian wood.'' [2]

All these natural resources could be had with little effort, he promised. Furthermore, with but little investment the area could produce silk, tobacco, and long-staple cotton. No doubt, had they read this, the starving, freezing, disease-ridden French settlers at Biloxi Bay four years later would have been puzzled over just what paradise Remonville was describing. Finally, the writer argued, if a French presence were not established in Louisiana, the ever-aggressive English traders along the Atlantic coast would undoubtedly press westward and pre-empt the French claims.

He proposed two alternatives. Parties of settlers could leave Canada following a route through the Great Lakes, down the Mississippi to establish a settlement near the mouth of the river. Perhaps, even better, a well-equipped expedition manned by both soldiers and settlers could sail directly from France and accomplish the same purpose. The king and his ministers chose the latter.

Placed in command was a thirty-seven-year-old French Canadian who as a North American explorer and military man already had achieved fame enough for a lifetime. Pierre Lemoyne

1. M. De Remonville, "Memoir on the Importance of Establishing a Colony in Louisiana'' (December 10, 1697), in *Historical Collections of Louisiana,* by B. F. French (New York: Wiley and Putnam, 1846), p. 2.

2. Remonville, "Memoir,'' p. 3.

d'Iberville combined the virtues the crown sought. He was an experienced sailor and military commander; as a native of the new world, he had tramped the backwoods, and he knew the wilderness and the Indians. Finally, he was a dedicated Anglophobe and wished to see England's presence in North America ended.

Through the summer of 1698, Iberville outfitted his force. He was given two thirty-gun ships, the *Badine* and the *Marin,* and two smaller vessels. Aboard these he loaded provisions, soldiers, and colonists. Iberville's instructions were simple and loose: he was to rendezvous his fleet at Santo Domingo, reprovision there, and pick up the *Francois,* a fifty-two-gun escort; then he was to proceed to the mouth of the Mississippi, select a site for a fort and settlement, and begin to map the area. Sites, routes, and other details were left to Iberville's discretion.

On October 24, 1698, Iberville's ships sailed from Brest. The stopover at Santo Domingo delayed them little, and by the end of January 1699, they arrived on the coast of Florida near the mouth of the Appalachicola River. Sailing to the west in search of an anchorage, they found the Spanish already situated at Pensacola Bay. Mobile Bay proved too shallow to enter. As Iberville paralleled the coast, off to starboard he saw what we know today as Dauphin, Petit Bois, and Horn, an island chain ten miles off the mainland. Finally he located, after much sounding from small boats, a satisfactory anchorage for his ships inside the western end of Ship Island. He was now twelve miles opposite Biloxi Bay.

His ships now safe from storms, Iberville immediately set about locating the mouth of the Mississippi. Loading a party in small boats, he felt his way westward. On March 2, he found the northernmost mouth of the Mississippi, North Pass. He entered in search of evidence that he had in fact found the mouth of the same river reported by La Salle nearly two decades earlier. For nearly a month the party rowed laboriously upriver, seeking proof that it was indeed the Mississippi. Although he had not yet found solid evidence, Iberville nevertheless was soon satisfied and began his descent southward. He split his party south of modern-day Baton Rouge, the main body to return to the Ship Island anchorage by retracing the route out the mouth of the river. Iberville and a few men in canoes took an Indian short cut through the Bayou Manchac, Lakes Maurepas and Pontchartrain, and the Rigolets, and thus into Mississippi Sound.

Upon his return to the anchorage at Ship Island, Iberville received irrefutable proof that he had ascended the same river navigated earlier by La Salle. His younger brother the Sieur de Bienville, a member of the party that had returned through the mouth of the river, located a French letter dated April 20, 1685, held by the Indians for fourteen years. In exchange for an axe, the Indians gave up the letter, which proved to be a message left by Henri de Tonty, a colleague of La Salle's who had made a trip downriver in search of his friend who was then lost on the Texas coast. Iberville now had proof that he was in the right place, and he set about finding a site for his fort and settlement. He took soundings in both the mouth of the Pascagoula River and at Biloxi Bay. Both places proved too shallow even for small vessels. As Iberville was about to move westward to establish his settlement on Lake Pontchartrain, he took a last sounding at Biloxi Bay and to his delight found a narrow channel of enough depth to accommodate small ships. Now running short of provisions, Iberville made his decision. He would leave his ships at the deep water anchorage near Ship Island and use his small boats to ferry settlers and provisions into Biloxi Bay. Iberville chose for the fort a site on the eastern bank of Biloxi Bay, now the modern city of Ocean Springs. Fort Maurepas, as Iberville named the fort, was complete by May 1699—a four-sided wooden palisade with a bastion at each corner. Iberville considered the Biloxi Bay site temporary—to be used so that "in the meantime, the place most convenient for the colony can be selected at leisure." [3]

The Biloxi Bay settlement proved not only temporary, as Iberville intended, but tenuous as well. After seeing the fort

3. M. P. Le Moyne d'Iberville, "Narrative of the Voyage Made by Order of the King of France in 1698 to take Possession of Louisiana," in *Historical Collections*, p. 30.

built and some subsistence crops planted, Iberville left in May to return to France, leaving the Sieur de Sauvole in charge. Appointed as Souvole's lieutenant was Iberville's younger brother Bienville. As commandant, Sauvole headed a garrison of seventy-six men. He had provisions for only six months.

From the time Iberville left for France in mid-1699 to 1702, when the Biloxi site was abandoned, the settlement all but died out. Disease took the greatest toll among the garrison. Those who escaped death often were too sick to work. Sauvole noted the effects of "tertian fever," probably malaria, in a letter to the authorities back in France. "Our sick," he reported, "who are of the number of thirty cannot recover from a tertian fever that saps their strength for lack of remedies. . . . The observation that I have made is that when the rain comes sickness is not long in coming also." [4] He lamented further, "I can only occupy our people two hours in the morning and two hours in the evening, because of the great heat. . . . The majority of our people have been hit with dysentery. The bad waters without doubt have caused it." [5]

To make matters worse, Iberville had planted his settlement on the most unproductive soil in the area. Leaders of the settlement in their letters to the authorities in France almost invariably remarked on the sterility of the soil at Biloxi. Sauvole complained, "In regard to the land, it is certainly unproductive. It is nothing but burning sand—our men have planted very often, and unprofitably." [6]

A later settler, M. Le Page du Pratz, came to Louisiana in 1718 to settle his grant at Natchez. By that time old Fort Maurepas had long been abandoned and New Biloxi established on the peninsula across the Bay. He saw the relocation as no great improvement.

4. Dunbar Rowland and Albert G. Sanders, editors, *Mississippi Provincial Archives, 1701–1729: French Dominion,* 3 vols. (Jackson, Mississippi: Press of the Mississippi Department of Archives and History, 1929): 2:12.

5. Jay Higginbotham, editor, *The Journal of Sauvole* (Mobile: Colonial Books, 1969), p. 27.

6. Higginbotham, *Journal of Sauvole,* p. 27.

> Biloxi is situate[d] opposite Ship-Island and four leagues from it. But I never could guess the reason, why the principal settlement was made at this place, nor why the capital should be built at it; as nothing could be more repugnant to good sense. . . . The land is the most barren of any to be found hereabouts; being nothing but a fine sand, as white and shining as snow, on which no kind of greens can be raised.[7]

He further remarked on the abundance of rats, which "ate even the stocks of the guns, the famine being so great," and noted that "more than five hundred people died of hunger." [8]

The result was that Biloxi relied almost exclusively for subsistence on game, on corn obtained from the neighboring Indians, and on supply ships from France. When the latter failed to appear on time, the settlers starved; or, weakened by hunger, they succumbed to the ever-present fever. Commandant Sauvole himself died from the fever in August of 1701, leaving in charge of the settlement the man whose name became more closely linked to the destinies of French Louisiana than any other—Jean Baptiste le Moyne, Sieur de Bienville, the younger brother of Iberville. Iberville did not return to the colony after 1701. He died of yellow fever at Havana in 1706.

By 1702 the French recognized the impossibility of keeping their principal settlement at Biloxi Bay. The focus of settlement now shifted to more fertile areas—first to Mobile Bay, a few miles to the east, and finally to New Orleans. That site was laid out by Bienville in 1718, and the capital moved there in 1722. The settlements at Biloxi, according to Du Pratz, went into a "deserved oblivion as lasting as their duration was short." [9]

Another site, perhaps more familiar in the history of Mississippi even than Biloxi, already fascinated the French. About 150 miles upriver from New Orleans, high bluffs on the eastern bank overlook the Mississippi. It is the first high country en-

7. Joseph G. Tregle, Jr., editor, *The History of Louisiana, Translated from the French of M. Le Page du Pratz* (1774; reprint ed., Baton Rouge: Louisiana State University Press, 1975), pp. 31–32.

8. Tregle, *History of Louisiana,* pp. 31–32.

9. Tregle, *History of Louisiana,* p. 50.

countered as one ascends the river. These bluffs formed the homeland of the Natchez Indians, a large and, the French would soon find, a fierce tribe. As early as 1701, Sauvole at Biloxi noted that he ordered four men to the Natchez country "fifty leagues from here" to "discover whether the country is good." They reported that it was "perfectly good and agreeable." [10]

It was not, however, until 1716 that the French established a permanent presence in the Natchez country. In 1714 and 1715 the Natchez, antagonized by the construction of a French trading post on their lands and by Governor Antoine de la Mothe Cadillac's refusal to parley, murdered several French traders and looted the trading post. Bienville, in charge of a small party of French troops, was sent to punish the Indians. From the French standpoint, he succeeded admirably. By trickery and bluff, he forced the execution of the perpetrators and demanded the return of the merchandise, horses, and slaves stolen from the French. Finally, he forced the Natchez to construct a fort to be occupied by the French.

Though the French later would have even more serious trouble with the Natchez, the peace dictated by Bienville and the construction of Fort Rosalie opened the Natchez area to French settlement. Natchez prospered as Biloxi had not. Situated on high bluffs above the Mississippi River, blessed with rich alluvial soil along the river and in the creek bottoms, Natchez did not face the twin problems of disease and sterile soil that had so plagued the settlement at Biloxi. The Superior of the Capuchin Mission in Louisiana wrote that

> The good quality of the land and the ease of clearing it together with the purity of the air are already attracting and will in the future attract many settlers to it . . . whereas on the lower part of the river one has continually to protect oneself against the floods and there are extremely dense forests to be cleared away. At the Natchez there are only weeds to be burned and never any flood . . . Tobacco grows there very well. Indigo will grow there. . . . I do not understand how . . . they have been able hitherto to disparage and

10. Roland and Sanders, *Mississippi Provincial Archives,* 2:16.

neglect a country at which one has only to glance to be charmed with it.[11]

By the standards of French Louisiana, Natchez after 1716 enjoyed dramatic growth. More than 300 settlers and slaves lived near Fort Rosalie by 1723. By 1729 the population had risen to more than 750. These new settlers cleared land and began to cultivate tobacco, wheat, indigo, silk, rice, timber, and hogs. The prospect of producing tobacco in commercial quantities particularly intrigued the French authorities. They hoped that Natchez tobacco would prove to be of a better quality than that of Virginia, and Louisiana could begin to break the new monopoly of the British on that commodity. So impressed with the growth and promise of Natchez were the French authorities that they designated Fort Rosalie as the headquarters of a new Natchez District, one of nine administrative subdivisions into which Louisiana was divided. The district formed a great triangle, its base stretching forty miles eastward from the Mississippi River along the thirty-first parallel and its apex near the mouth of the Yazoo River.

Just as Natchez seemed on the verge of eclipsing other Louisiana settlements, trouble, never completely eliminated, reemerged with the Natchez Indians. From their first contacts with the Natchez, the French complained of the Indians' arrogance, shrewdness, and independence. Perhaps more than other Indians, the Natchez resisted the attempts of French missionaries to introduce Christianity and European morality. Most important of all, they objected to the ever-growing French presence on their lands.

Trouble erupted once more in 1722. The Natchez, increasingly resentful of French encroachments that threatened even their sacred grand village on Saint Catherine's Creek, made war. Again Bienville, now governor and now needing five hundred troops, not the thirty-four required in 1716, destroyed two Natchez villages and dictated peace. Earlier, French au-

11. Roland and Sanders, *Mississippi Provincial Archives,* 2:527.

thorities had predicted that nothing short of annihilation would remove the problem of the Natchez.

The showdown came in 1729. A new, arrogant, and arbitrary commandant at Fort Rosalie, the Sieur de Chepart, not only demanded from the Indians the lands on which their main village stood, but also ordered them to bring him free provisions monthly and to make preparations to remove themselves from the area. The Natchez refused to be pressed further. Conspiring with their neighbors, the Yazoo and Chickasaw to the north, the Indians all agreed to rise simultaneously and to eliminate the French both from Natchez and from all of their interior posts east of the Mississippi. The time agreed upon was the end of 1729. The Natchez, fearful that the plot had been discovered, rose early. Indeed, Chepart had received word a number of days before that the Natchez would attempt to slaughter the settlers of Natchez and the soldiers of the garrison, but he discounted the information and refused to make preparations on the questionable theory that the Indians would interpret such precautions as a sign of weakness.

On November 29, 1729, under the pretext of delivering the monthly provisions and of borrowing guns to go hunting, the Natchez managed to infiltrate Fort Rosalie and the cabins of most of the settlers. The slaughter was general. The Indians killed nearly three hundred Frenchmen before noon. They took more than four hundred women and slaves captive. These, the Natchez hoped, could be enslaved and held for ransom. Moreover, the Indians hoped the captives as hostages, would protect them from French retribution. A month later, on January 1, 1730, the Yazoos dealt similarly with the settlers and the garrison at Fort Saint Peter, the French post near the mouth of the Yazoo River. Only a handful escaped this second slaughter. The Natchez district was decimated. One of the most promising settlements in French Louisiana was suddenly swept away. Although the French returned with an army and for two years hunted the Natchez to complete destruction, the Natchez settlements could not be revived. Haunted by memories of the massacre, plagued by an increasing lack of interest from France and New Orleans, French forces manned the Natchez bluffs through the remainder of the history of French Louisiana only with a small number of French soldiers on outpost duty in a decaying fort.

France found her colony of Louisiana unrewarding. For more than sixty years the French controlled the area that was eventually to become the state of Mississippi. They made little impact. After the Natchez War of 1729–1730, the only French settlements of any consequence lay along the Gulf Coast, where Iberville started, six decades before; even there, the coastal settlements stretching from the Bay of Saint Louis to the Pascagoula River lived in the shadow of the more important cities of New Orleans and Mobile.

2

Enter the British

IN the August heat of 1763, Lieutenant Colonel Augustine Prevost, commanding the Third Battalion of Britain's Royal American Regiment, stepped ashore on the white sands of Pensacola Bay. A month later, 664 Spaniards and 108 Roman Catholic Indians sailed out of the bay for Vera Cruz. On October 20, Major Robert Farmer, after stopping briefly at Jamaica and Pensacola, took possession of Mobile. Those two events in 1763 represented the culmination of a hundred-year struggle for control of North America. When the final phase of this great struggle between Britain and France for North America began in 1754, the prizes were the Ohio Valley and New France in the Saint Lawrence valley. Louisiana, in the lower Mississippi valley seemed to be only a negotiating pawn. By 1759 France realized that the French and Indian War was lost, and hence, her North American empire. Rather than see all of Louisiana, along with Canada, go to her enemy, Britain, France in 1762 ceded all of French Louisiana to her ally Spain. In turn, at Paris in 1763, Spain ceded to Britain that part of Louisiana east of the Mississippi except for the Isle of Orleans. In the same settlement, Britain received East Florida. Thus by 1763 the Mississippi River divided Spanish North America from British North America.

The British Board of Trade earlier had given little consideration to their new possessions in East Florida and eastern Louisiana. The government was largely ignorant of its new territories. In fact, the ministers had been pelted with criticism for taking these seemingly worthless lands in preference to some of the French possessions in the West Indies. The observations of Lieutenant Colonel Prevost and Major Farmer seemed to corroborate the critics. Neither Mobile nor Pensacola gave the appearance of more than sixty years of settlement. The buildings, both public and private, were hardly more than board shacks with roofs of thatched palmetto leaves. Mobile, noted an early British report, was a remarkably unhealthful, fever-ridden place. Pensacola, the new occupants wrote, seemed somewhat more wholesome.

Yet, like the French before them, the British soon appreciated the potential promise of their newly acquired lands. Pitch, tar, and timber would provide stores for the British navy, now the foremost in the world. After establishing settlers in the interior, the British predicted indigo, tobacco, and other profitable crops could be produced with little effort.

But the problems of administration and government came first. Out of her newly acquired lands, which stretched from Hudson Bay to the Gulf of Mexico, Great Britain constructed three new North American colonies—Canada, East Florida, and West Florida. The government reserved the vast interior from the Appalachians to the Mississippi for the Indians.

The new colony of West Florida was bounded on the west by the Mississippi River, on the east by the Appalachicola River, on the south by the Gulf of Mexico, and on the north by the northern shores of Lakes Maurepas and Pontchartrain and at 31° north latitude. Finding shortly that 31° north latitude left the fertile areas in the river valleys north of Mobile and the rich Mississippi River lands north of Baton Rouge beyond the boundaries of the colony, the British Board of Trade in 1764 moved the northern boundary to 32°28′ north latitude, a line from the mouth of the Yazoo River on the west to the Chattahoochee River on the east.

The British set the capital at Pensacola. The colony was to be administered by a royal governor and council. However, they had few to govern. Pensacola had been virtually abandoned by the

Spanish. Only a few Frenchmen remained around Mobile; Biloxi had long before shrunk into insignificance, inhabited only by a few descendants of the original French settlers. These eked a livelihood from grazing cattle and making pitch and tar. The Mississippi River bank from Baton Rouge north to the Walnut Hills was largely unsettled since the Natchez war with the French three decades before. Hence, the British, in addition to the job of establishing a colonial government, had, largely, to build a colony through land grants, to place inhabitants, and to make the colony productive.

The British recognized, as the French had earlier, the importance of the now vacant Natchez area. During the spring of 1768 Lieutenant Governor Montfort Browne began a journey of inspection into the western part of the colony along the banks of the Mississippi. He went by the route that the British later would habitually use to maintain communication and trade between Pensacola and Mobile and their thriving settlements along the Mississippi. It was the same short cut d'Iberville discovered nearly seventy years before. The route, which ran through Mississippi Sound and the Rigolets, through Lakes Pontchartrain and Maurepas, and out the Amite and Iberville rivers into the Mississippi a few miles south of Baton Rouge, not only was more direct, but allowed the British to bypass Spanish-held New Orleans. Lieutenant Governor Browne, upon arriving at the Natchez Bluffs, was so impressed that he declared he would be content to live there for the rest of his days. Thomas Hutchins, a geographer who examined the area before taking up lands there, likewise noted the remarkable agreeableness of the Natchez region. "The soil at this place," he observed, "is superior to any . . . on the borders of the river Mississippi. . . ." It would, he predicted, produce abundant crops of "Indian corn, rice, hemp, flax, indigo, cotton, pot-herbs . . . and pasturage; and the tobacco made here is esteemed preferable to any cultivated in other parts of America." Moreover, the climate was healthful because "the elevated, open, airy, situation of the country renders it less liable to fevers and agues." [1]

[1] Cecil Johnson, *British West Florida, 1763–1783* (New Haven: Yale University Press, 1943), p. 157.

British authorities endorsed an extremely liberal land policy for West Florida. Every head of household could claim one hundred acres for himself and fifty for each member of his household, including slaves. Veterans of the French and Indian War could claim large grants—five thousand acres for field-grade officers, three thousand for captains, two thousand for subalterns or staff officers, two hundred for noncommissioned officers, and fifty for privates. In addition to these, through influence in the colony or with the crown in England, favored individuals could gain huge tracts of fertile soil. Among the first grants in the Natchez area in 1766 were twenty thousand acres to the Earl of Eglinton, two thousand to Daniel Clark, and five thousand to Samuel Hannay of London, all by royal order. In 1767 and 1768, grants in the area became more numerous, but more reasonable in size, ranging from two hundred to two thousand acres.

Other than the obvious fertility of the soil and the comparatively healthful climate, other factors also attracted settlers to the Natchez area. Fertile land was increasingly scarce in the Atlantic colonies. Opportunities for land speculation attracted others. Still others saw opportunity for trade, both legal and illegal; a thriving illegal trade soon developed with the Spanish in New Orleans and across the river. But most immigrants came for the same reason people historically followed the frontier—opportunity. As on all frontiers, too, some settlers succeeded and others failed.

One who succeeded was Anthony Hutchins. Many British loyalists, driven from the Atlantic states by the Revolution, sought refuge in West Florida in the early 1770s, and Hutchins was among them. A retired British captain, he was a brother to Thomas Hutchins, the geographer who had earlier noted the fertility of Natchez. Already a substantial planter and local political power in North Carolina, Anthony Hutchins traveled to Natchez in 1772 to lay claim to one thousand acres. His subsequent career as a Natchez planter, while perhaps not typical, reflects the tenacity, courage, single-mindedness, and ability to overcome adversity that were necessary to make a success in the Mississippi wilderness. Already nearly sixty years old when he set out with his family to float the Tennessee, Ohio, and Mississippi rivers into the new country, Hutchins overcame, in the next twenty-five years, Indian attacks, law suits, revolts, and two changes of government before his death in 1804. By then, he was a controversial community leader and one of the most influential and prosperous frontier planters in the Natchez District. A Loyal British subject when he came to Natchez, he saw his wilderness land pass from the hands of the British to the Spanish in 1779 and from Spain to the United States in 1798.

First inclined to settle on Saint Catherine's Creek, Hutchins, according to one story, fell in with an Indian who led him on foot through the woods and canebrakes to a pastoral tract sixteen miles south of Natchez on Second Creek—the site of the previous Natchez Indian settlement of White Apple Village.

In 1773, Hutchins and several of his associates had reserved for them by the West Florida Colonial Council 152,000 acres, provided that they bring in as residents on the tract settlers from Virginia and the Carolinas.

When Hutchins moved onto his claim at White Apple Village, the area had not been cultivated since the Natchez Indians had been driven from the site by the French three decades before. Frontier fashion, the Hutchins family set about clearing the land, building cabins, and planting subsistence crops. Hutchins soon saw his first buildings and crops razed by an Indian attack. But he returned, and by 1779 his land holdings approached two thousand acres; he had begun to produce subsistence crops such as vegetables and corn and the staple cash crops of the day, tobacco and livestock. Like most rising frontiersmen, Hutchins was interested in land both for planting and for speculation. He bought and sold land with some regularity, either to turn a profit or to settle members of his family on it.

Small and lean in stature, outspoken to the point of irascibility, Hutchins was a natural leader in political and military affairs. Like many of his neighbors, he opposed the American Revolution and organized opposition in the district to supporters of the rebels. When the Spanish declared war on Britain and attacked Natchez in 1779, Hutchins organized resistance to them also. When his efforts failed and the Spanish conquered the Natchez District—and, by 1781, the rest of West Florida—Hutchins fled to Georgia, sure that the Spanish would at least confiscate his property, if not hang him. But the Spanish were lenient; he was allowed to keep his property, and he returned to White Apple Village to become even more prosperous.

In 1789, his holdings produced more than 22,000 pounds of tobacco, which he sold for $1,768. When the Spanish gave up the district to the United States, Hutchins, with crops of indigo, cotton, and tobacco, and a herd of cattle numbering more than a thousand head, was one of the three or four largest landholders and planters along the Mississippi.

As a frontiersman, Hutchins was perhaps more typical than would at first appear. He was part soldier and part politician and partly driven by a spirit of adventure. He persevered and overcame hardships to gain land and wealth. He fought, first against the American Revolutionists, then against the Spanish, not primarily for political ideals, but to protect his property and his family. If he was often irascible and litigious—he once brought suit in court to recover a saddle from a neighbor and two suits to recover a barrel of flour—it was because, in true frontier tradition, he was zealously protective of his rights. When he died in 1804, in his mid-eighties, he left a clan of kin and a small empire. Yet he never lived in a white-columned mansion, nor did he ever own more than a few slaves. These accouterments of Natchez awaited another generation.

Frontier Natchez also produced its disasters—men who came with great expectations and were broken by the wilderness. Matthew Phelps was a New Englander from Connecticut who journeyed to the Natchez district in 1773, only a year after Anthony Hutchins had come to inspect his claim at White Apple Village. Phelps kept a journal of his experiences. Insight into his attempts to settle his claim on the banks of the Big Black River in the northern part of the Natchez District may be gained from the introduction to his journal. It was written, he said, "That the story may prove consoling to some under the pressures of misfortune . . . and of inducing more to feel that wretches feel, and to drop the tear of sympathy for woes that know no remedy. . . ." [2] He described a four-year catalogue

2. Anthony Haswell, *Memoirs and Adventures of Captain Matthew Phelps* (Bennington, Vermont: Anthony Haswell, 1802), pp. 7–8.

of catastrophes that broke him and sent him disheartened back to his native New England.

The son of a struggling farmer, Phelps moved as a young man to Norfolk, Vermont, where he became a moderately successful tradesman, until his wife became seriously ill, and he developed consumption. When his physician advised an ocean voyage to restore Phelps's health, the young man decided to couple a recuperative voyage with an inspection of lands in the Natchez District, of which he had heard good reports. As a veteran of the French and Indian War, he was entitled to a grant.

In December 1773 he set sail from Stonington, Connecticut, bound for New Orleans. He arrived in good health and high spirits. With the company of several other potential settlers, his party hired boats and journeyed uneventfully up the Mississippi to inspect the lands north of Natchez along the Big Black River. He was much impressed. The fertility of the soil and the friendliness of the settlers were only offset by Phelps's worries about the unwholesome climate. Convinced now that he should move his family to the new land, Phelps took up a claim, paid the necessary fifty dollars, and arranged for two friends to look after it until his return. He planned to return to New England directly, sell his property, and bring his family to the Big Black. As he returned downriver, at New Orleans, he was felled momentarily by fever—only a portent of what was to come.

Upon his return to New England, Phelps temporarily gave up his dream of immigrating to the new country, because of the onset of the American Revolution. But in 1775 his determination returned, and with his now-pregnant wife and his three children—Ruth, Abigail, and Luman—he made plans. The oldest child, Ruth, was ten, and Luman, the youngest, six. Despite Mrs. Phelps's pregnancy, the family embarked for New Orleans on May 1, 1776. Off both Long Island and Florida, their ship eluded British men-of-war; for more than a week, they lay becalmed in the Gulf of Mexico, short of food and water. Six days from the mouth of the Mississippi, with the aid of other female passengers, Jerusha Phelps gave birth to a son, promptly named Atlantic by the ship's crew.

In early August Phelps and his family finally reached New

Orleans. There they paused only long enough to get boats and provisions for the journey upriver. Together with two other New England families, the Joseph Leonards and the Josiah Flowerses, they set out for the Big Black. Only Phelps eventually made it. They had only reached Manchac, a short way upriver from New Orleans, when fever struck Phelps and his eldest daughter Ruth. A few days later his wife Jerusha, daughter Abigail, and infant son Atlantic contracted the fever. Three days later Luman was seized with it. Forced to stop temporarily, they slowly recovered sufficiently to continue upstream. They left the Flowerses behind at Point Coupee, north of Baton Rouge. There Mrs. Flowers shortly died. The Leonards were left behind at Natchez, where Mrs. Leonard died. Stopping again temporarily to regain strength, the Phelps family pressed on. On September 16 Phelps's daughter Abigail died. Ten days later Atlantic died. After burying his children, Phelps, with his wife and two remaining children, struggled on northward to Petit Gulf. There on October 14 Mrs. Phelps died.

Finally Phelps, his daughter Ruth, and son Luman reached the Big Black. Now too weak to continue, Phelps hired a man and boy to take him up the Big Black to his claim. Unable to row against the swift current, Phelps and his two hired men left the children in the boat and stepped ashore and began pulling the boat upriver by rope. Hardly had they gone three miles before disaster struck once more. A partly submerged willow obstructed the channel, and against it debris had accumulated to create a dangerous whirlpool. The boat wedged against the fallen tree and began to sink. Phelps managed to wind his tow rope fast to a tree and crawled out on the fallen willow to rescue his children. His weight broke the tree loose; the boat broke free and capsized. He watched as his two remaining children drowned—their bodies, his provisions, and boat swept downriver. Phelps, too, had fallen in and, although he could not swim, managed to struggle ashore. Phelps sent his two hired men downstream to search for the boat and his children's bodies while he struggled, freezing, through the woods toward the nearest settlement. On the verge of death from exposure, he was rescued by two men from a nearby plantation.

The ordeal was not over yet. On November 29, 1776, Phelps at last arrived at his property—only to discover that his claim was forfeited for nonsettlement. Taken in by John Storrs and son, two men he had befriended on his first trip in 1773, Phelps was nursed back to health and staked to a new claim. Financially broken, with no provisions or implements, Phelps persevered. Just as he began to recover physically and financially, Phelps's life once more was disrupted, this time by backwoods events that grew out of the American Revolution. He joined the British army, and for three years he helped to defend Natchez. After the Spanish, at war with Britain since 1779, captured Natchez in 1780, Matthew Phelps gave up in despair and returned from whence he came. Back in Connecticut, he married the widow of Thankful Moore, moved to Vermont, had a new family of three children, and supported himself to a ripe old age by "honest labor" [3] in the more congenial surroundings of New England.

The American Revolution hardly touched the settlements along the eastern banks of the Mississippi before 1778. In fact, the Natchez area of British West Florida served as a haven for loyalists. Many supporters of the king who left or were driven from the Atlantic states by patriot pressure journeyed to the banks of the Mississippi to take up lands and continued to live under the Union Jack. Concerned with the problems of the frontier, they had little time for or interest in the events transpiring in the east.

In 1778 their peace and parochial concerns were shattered abruptly. Natchez's revolutionary troubles began when some members of the American Continental Congress saw merit in a plan to send a military expedition down the Mississippi. Supporters hoped such a venture could produce two results: it might persuade the planters along the lower Mississippi to desert their British allegiance and bring West Florida to the side of the Revolution; at the least, it would promote liaison with the sympathetic Spaniards in New Orleans, and supplies could be ferried upriver to aid the rebels in the east.

3. Haswell, *Memoirs of Captain Phelps*, p. 210.

Chosen to head the expedition was James Willing, a young man who earlier had spent some time as a Natchez trader and hence knew the country. Armed with a commission as captain in the United States Navy, Willing and twenty-nine men boarded the armed river boat *Rattletrap* at Fort Pitt and drifted out into the Ohio River on January 11, 1778. On February 18 they reached the northernmost settlements of the Natchez District. Here began a campaign by Willing that not only failed to bring most of the settlers over to the American side but hardened their loyalties to the British crown. Willing accepted the few settlers who wished to join the American cause. Those who took an oath of neutrality, Willing promised, would not be molested. Those settlers who persisted in their loyalty to the crown or who had incurred Willing's enmity when he lived at Natchez earlier saw their plantations looted and destroyed, their possessions and slaves hauled away southward to be sold by Willing in New Orleans. Most of the settlers around Natchez saved their possessions by taking the oath of neutrality, but Willing proved ruthless in his plunder and destruction downriver at the settlements of Point Coupee and Manchac.

After Willing reached New Orleans, he sent a small detachment back upriver to Natchez. Hearing of the plunder downriver, this time the Natchez settlers fought. In an ambush led by Hutchins and participated in by Phelps at Ellis's Cliffs south of Natchez, Lieutenant Reuben Harrison of the Willing expedition and four of his troops were killed outright. The other twenty-eight were captured.

Although Spain was still at peace with Great Britain, Governor Bernardo de Galvez sympathetically received Willing and his remaining men at New Orleans. The Spanish governor allowed Willing to dispose of his loot at public auctions and to make contact with an American merchant, Oliver Pollock, who was to furnish the provisions and military supplies for Willing to take back upriver.

Tactically daring and successful, Willing's raid was strategically a failure. He so frightened the British authorities at Pensacola and so alienated the settlers along the river that he could accomplish neither of his original objectives. The British reaction made him in effect a prisoner at New Orleans. Before he could proceed back upriver, the British mustered militia units at Natchez and Manchac and reinforced the forts with British regulars. The ill-fated Matthew Phelps gave up farming and enlisted as a corporal at Fort Panmure in Natchez. Remnants of Willing's force eventually made it back to the east by marching overland through Spanish Louisiana. Willing himself was captured by the British in 1778 aboard a private vessel in the Gulf of Mexico as he tried to return to Pennsylvania. He languished for the next three years in a prisoner-of-war camp on Long Island before eventually being exchanged in 1781.

As the Willing threat subsided, a far greater menace to British West Florida was rising, one that portended the loss of the entire colony. France joined the American colonies in their war with Britain in 1778. For months, British officials in West Florida feared that Spain would do the same. Should that happen, the British faced grave problems in the defense of West Florida. With only weakly held posts at Natchez, Manchac, Mobile, and Pensacola; with her Indian allies uncertain; and with the Spanish holding the more populous and larger possessions of New Orleans and Louisiana—Britain, already pressed by a world war, was in little position to defend West Florida with great vigor. Both governors, Peter Chester at Pensacola and Bernardo de Galvez at New Orleans, maintained a correct if suspicious relationship, while both made plans to attack across the Mississippi should war occur. In the summer of 1779, it did. The war between Britain and Spain arose mainly from European considerations. Neither nation devoted great resources to the conflict in the lower Mississippi Valley; neither considered the oncoming struggle between British West Florida and Spanish Louisiana a life-or-death struggle.

When war came, Governor Galvez moved more boldly than Governor Chester. Though the forts at Natchez, Manchac, Mobile, and Pensacola had been refurbished and reinforced, none was capable of withstanding the efficient and rapid onslaught mounted by Galvez. War was declared by Spain on June 21. News did not arrive at Pensacola until September. On September 3, Galvez, at the head of an army of regulars, militia, armed slaves, and Indians, was already marching toward Manchac and Baton Rouge. In three weeks, he seized Manchac and Baton Rouge, almost bloodlessly, and forced the surrender of Fort Panmure at Natchez. In March 1780 he took Fort Charlotte at Mobile and in May 1781 Fort George at Pensacola. The Natchez District once more changed hands, this time not at the negotiating table, as in 1763, but by armed conquest.

Spain had conquered a colony in which hardly a Spaniard lived and only a few Frenchmen. Especially in the Natchez District, the population was almost wholly British. At Natchez the settlers feared Spanish rule, and in May 1781 they made an abortive attempt to retake Fort Panmure from the Spanish. Momentarily they succeeded. Tricking the commander of the Spanish garrison into thinking that the fort was mined, settlers led by loyalist John Blommart forced the garrison to surrender. Scarcely had success come when word arrived that Pensacola had fallen to Spain. With that, the rebellion collapsed and the insurgents sought accommodation with the Spanish. A few diehards escaped to Indian territory, and Blommart and a few supporters were arrested, imprisoned, and eventually, in 1783, expelled from the colony. But the settlers' fears of Spanish harshness proved groundless. No wholesale vengeance followed. The Spanish ordered no executions. No confiscations occurred. The generally lenient treatment that the Natchez insurgents experienced previewed fifteen years of efficient and light-handed Spanish rule over an Anglo-American population.

The land that the Spanish had conquered was thoroughly anglicized. Travelers in the 1780s and 1790s remarked that one could journey through the Natchez District and, except for a few soldiers and administrators, find hardly a Spaniard and but few Frenchmen. Almost all settlers were by then Anglo-American. They numbered 1,619 people, including 498 slaves. Natchez proper was hardly more than a village. The settlers lived scattered along the river and creek bottoms for thirty miles north and south of the bluffs—from Bayou Pierre in the north to the Homochitto River in the south. None lived in ostentatious splendor. Plank or log houses served for the pillared mansions of later years, puncheon tables and chairs served the place of imported furniture. Indian corn, game, and dried meat were the common fare, and whisky substituted for Madeira. As late as 1797, English travelers, admittedly perhaps over-critical and used to more comforts, remarked on the primitive conditions and the lack of amenities that travelers were forced to suffer. While Francis Baily predicted a prosperous future and "progress of the arts of civilized life" for the Natchez District, he lamented the lack of "the luxuries or even the conveniences of life." Somewhat condescendingly, he observed, "a log house built upon their plantation, which is in general worked by negro slaves, together with a few cattle and articles of husbandry, forms their chief treasure." Because of the lack of inns, his travels had to be timed for him to arrive before nightfall at a dwelling, where

> a poor hut was our only shelter, and we were obliged to unpack our horses ourselves and turn them into the pasture; and if we could get a mess of *mush* and milk, some fried bacon, or some fresh meat of any kind, it was as much as we expected, and for this we were charged enormously high. . . . Our bed was . . . a hard floor, on which we would strew our blankets and lie till morning.[4]

Because such cabins were invariably "nest[s] of filth and dirt," he preferred taking his meager fare outside, "under the shade of some tree on the banks of some brook and eat it in cleanliness and comfort."[5] No doubt one could omit the reference to slaves and be left with a fitting description of any settlement on the far reaches of the American frontier.

Spain's conquest of British West Florida needed only to be confirmed in 1783 at the Paris negotiations that ended the wars of the American Revolution. Therein lay confusion. In preliminary articles between Britain and the United States, signed in 1782, Britain handed over to her former colonies the lands between the Appalachians and the Mississippi south to the 31° parallel, the original northern boundary of West Florida. But in 1764, a year after she took possession of West Florida, Britain

4. Francis Baily, *Journal of a Tour in Unsettled Parts of North America in 1796 and 1797*, edited by Jack D. L. Holmes (Carbondale: Southern Illinois Press, 1969), pp. 200–201.

5. Baily, *Journal of a Tour*, pp. 200–201.

had moved the northern boundary to 32°28′. In her treaty with Spain in 1783, Britain ceded West Florida without reference to the northern boundary. The result of that oversight was significant. Between 31° and 32°28′, from the Mississippi on the west to the Chattahoochee, the lands in which the highly desirable Natchez settlements were paramount came into dispute, claimed by both Spain and the United States. In fact, the area was also claimed by the state of Georgia, which created in 1785 the stillborn county of Bourbon. Yet Spain had the Natchez District by conquest, and the United States, short of war, could only protest diplomatically.

From 1779 to 1788, the commandant of the Spanish garrison at Natchez performed the business of government, combining his military duties with such civil functions as the administration of justice, the enforcement of regulations and laws, and the preservation of law and order. That Spaniards were scarce in the district is indicated by the appointment in 1781 of Stephen Minor, a native of Pennsylvania, as post adjutant. In that capacity, he served as the commandant's and governor's chief assistant until 1797, when he was named Spain's last governor of the Natchez District. Late in 1788, the Natchez area had so grown in population that the Spanish crown appointed Manuel Luis Gayoso de Lemos y Amorin as governor. In that capacity, Gayoso was responsible, as the commandants before him had been, to the Governor General for Spanish Louisiana at New Orleans.

Gayoso's appointment was auspicious for both the Spanish authorities and the Natchez settlers. In the Mississippi valley, Spain confronted directly the bumptious new American nation. If she provoked the Natchez settlers, she risked driving them into the arms of the United States and producing disaffection in all of Louisiana or, at worst, provoking war with the United States. Fluent in English, married to an American wife, devoted to lavish entertainment and diplomatically ingratiating, Gayoso proved the ideal administrator for Spanish policy in the Natchez District. So masterfully did he perform that in 1797 the Spanish authorities promoted him to the post of Governor General of Louisiana.

The Spaniards understood from the outset the futility of attempting to displace the Anglo-American population and settling Spaniards in their places. Thus Spain's policy aimed at making loyal Spanish subjects of the Anglo-American settlers and, through liberal land grants and the promotion of agriculture, attracting more Americans into the area. The plan worked for almost twenty years, and when Spain finally acceded to the United States's claims to the Natchez area, it was more because of international problems than from any burning desire of the Natchez inhabitants to free themselves from Spanish rule.

A proclamation issued by the governor general at New Orleans in 1789 invited Americans to settle at Natchez. They would, he assured them, receive lands. He promised they could bring their property into the colony duty free. Nor would Protestants be prohibited. No settler, he assured them, "would be molested on religious matters." [6] Only two reservations did he make: settlers must take an oath of allegiance to the Spanish crown and swear to defend the province should it be attacked; and only the Roman Catholic faith could be publicly exercised. Private Protestant worship would be permitted. Spain allowed such leniencies to no other colony.

Spain attracted the allegiance of the older settlers by appealing to their strongest traits—the desires to accumulate more land and to make money. Liberal land grants were offered to old and new settlers alike. Spanish authorities only stipulated that improvements be made on the land and that it actually be occupied. If the grantee failed to fulfill these obligations, the land reverted to the crown. Nor would grants be made for speculation, an obvious attempt to attract settlers instead of enriching speculators. Older settlers like Anthony Hutchins saw their domains enlarge considerably by additional Spanish grants.

Certainly the most immediately profitable and popular Spanish policy was the tobacco subsidy. Although tobacco was produced in the Natchez region as early as the French period, neither in quality nor quantity had Natchez tobacco rivaled that of Virginia. Spanish authorities granted the Natchez planters a

6. Jack D. L. Holmes, *Gayoso: The Life of a Spanish Governor in the Mississippi Valley, 1789–1799* (Baton Rouge: Louisiana State University Press, 1965), p. 34.

guaranteed market at New Orleans for their tobacco at a price of ten dollars per hundredweight, a sum far in excess of the world price. Under this stimulus, dramatic results followed. In 1786 the Natchez crop totalled 590,000 pounds. In 1789 the Natchez planters produced almost 1.5 million pounds. But like their descendants, who later planted cotton, the planters found that the tobacco boom was momentary. No longer able to bear the expense in 1790, the Spanish crown ordered tobacco purchases limited to 40,000 pounds. To soothe the outraged planters, the Spanish authorities agreed to a temporary moratorium on debts that the Natchez planters owed to the New Orleans merchants. With the subsidy eliminated, by 1796, Natchez hardly produced enough tobacco to fill its own needs.

Indigo had long been an important crop at Natchez, and after processing, the dye sold for up to $2.50 per pound. But processing the plant into the finished product required lengthy, cumbersome, and unhealthful labor. The crop also suffered periodic insect devastation, and the price for the finished product fluctuated considerably. For these reasons, indigo production never assumed the scale of tobacco agriculture and by 1794 passed from the Natchez scene entirely. Increasing evidence indicates that the Natchez planters in this period relied heavily on the production of livestock, both for their own needs and for export. In 1784 the Natchez area counted 3,000 head of cattle. By 1792 cattle numbered more than 15,000, and those features that we normally associate with the nineteenth-century West already were well established at Natchez—the annual roundup, open grazing on public lands, brands, and trail drives.

The commodity that so marked the future of the lower South moved into Mississippi's history late in the Spanish period. Before 1795 some Natchez planters grew cotton, but hardly on a commercial scale. As early as the 1720s, the French experimented along the Gulf Coast with Sea Island Cotton—a perennial, treelike plant with long-stapled lint that adhered loosely to a large black seed. But the Sea Island variety was marginal, even that far north. Georgia Upland or Green-Seed cotton, introduced into the uplands of the Atlantic South early in the eighteenth century, also seemed unsuitable, because of its short staple, its hard green seed, and the difficulty encountered in separating lint from seeds. Because early French settlers lost their Sea Island plants to frost, in 1733 French settlers imported a Siamese variety. It seemed to thrive and remained the chief variety of cotton in the lower Mississippi valley until the early nineteenth century. Known as Black-Seed, or Creole cotton, the Siamese strain embodied the advantages of Sea Island cotton without its drawbacks. It also had a large black seed and produced a fine white lint only slightly shorter in staple than Sea Island. Creole cotton had to be replanted annually, whereas Sea Island cotton was a perennial. The lint could be separated from the seed in small quantities with the primitive roller gins then in use. On rich bottom lands, one could produce as much as two thousand pounds of seed cotton to the acre—so much that the roller gins could not keep pace.

To this variety Natchez planters turned in 1795, after the failure of tobacco and indigo culture. Had they tried expanding cotton production five years earlier, no doubt they would have failed. But by 1795, the Whitney gin, developed for the hard-to-separate Georgia upland cotton, became known in the Natchez region. In the summer of 1795, on the plantation of Daniel Clark, Sr., three men—James Bolls, Jr., the son of a neighboring planter; a mechanic named Hughes; and John Barclay, recently returned from Georgia where he may have seen the Whitney machine—built a gin following Whitney's design. They made one modification. Instead of the iron wires mounted on rollers and rotating through slots, they substituted saws, a revision that persists into the present. Within three years, virtually every Natchez planter of consequence built a similar device. The main bottleneck of cotton agriculture was removed. Rotated by a horse, the modified Whitney gin could process five hundred to fifteen hundred pounds of lint daily. The rush to cotton in the Natchez District was in motion, soon to mold the history of the whole state. If cotton saved the Natchez planters from economic ruin, it also invigorated its handmaiden—slavery.

The first black slaves were brought to what is now Mississippi by the French. Even as the first French settlers began to move to the Natchez bluffs after 1716, they competed keenly for blacks who were imported by the authorities. Perhaps as great as the southern frontier settler's hunger for cheap land was his desire for slave labor to help him work it. Numerous letters written by French and British administrators to their governments in Paris or London emphasize the necessity for importing more slaves. Both tobacco and indigo culture favored slave labor, but the transition to cotton production made slavery even more widespread. In 1784 the Spanish census showed 498 slaves in the Natchez District. By 1798 that number quintupled to approximately 2,400. The white population in the same year numbered about 4,500.

By the mid-1790s Spain's policy toward the Natchez District was undergoing a dramatic reversal. The driving force behind Spain's shift lay both in threats to Louisiana from the American settlements in Kentucky and in the momentous events then sweeping Europe as a result of the French Revolution. The Kentuckians, irate at Spanish control of the Mississippi and the port of New Orleans, threatened invasion. Also the egalitarian ideals of the Revolution infected many Frenchmen living under Spanish rule in Louisiana. Momentarily, the Spanish Governor General of Louisiana, Baron de Hector Carondelet, dealt with the United States General James Wilkinson, who claimed that, with enough Spanish money, he could organize a separatist movement in the western American settlements. Convincingly, Wilkinson argued that the Kentucky settlements had lost faith in the United States government's ability to extract concessions from Spain regarding navigation of the Mississippi and the use of the Port of New Orleans. The Spanish decision was clear—she could risk war with the United States by supporting Wilkinson, or she could negotiate her differences with the new American nation. In any case, Spain was compelled by military and financial commitments to the wars of the French Revolution in Europe to solve her problems with the United States. She chose the course of negotiation. At stake were not only her differences with the United States concerning navigation of the Mississippi and the use of the port of New Orleans by Americans in the western settlements, but also the old dispute from 1783 regarding ownership of the Natchez District—the lands between 32°28′ and 31° north latitude. So pressed was Spain that she surrendered on all points. On October 27, 1795, at the monastery of San Lorenzo outside Madrid, Manuel de Godoy, chief minister of Spain, and Thomas Pinckney, United States Minister to Great Britain, signed the Treaty of San Lorenzo. By its terms, Americans were given the rights of free navigation on the Mississippi and free use of the port of New Orleans. Most important for the future of the state of Mississippi, however, Spain validated the American claim to the lands between 32°28′ and 31° north latitude. The district prepared for yet another transfer of power, this time into the United States of America.

The shift of the Natchez District from Spanish to United States control stretched on longer and promoted perhaps as much controversy as the negotiation of the treaty that mandated the transferral. For almost three years after the signing of the Treaty of San Lorenzo, the Natchez inhabitants found themselves in governmental limbo and in a tangle of conflicting loyalities, personality conflicts, and power struggles.

Hardly had the Spanish authorities signed the treaty before they had second thoughts. The possibility of stimulating further the western secessionist ambitions of the Kentuckians still existed. Governor General Carondelet at New Orleans personally opposed the concessions in the treaty. Most important of all it appeared to Spain that Britain had ambitions in the Mississippi valley that directly threatened Louisiana. Hence by late 1796 Spain determined to delay her evacuation of the posts in the Natchez District, principally Fort Nogales (Walnut Hills) and Natchez.

In February 1797, after an icy float down the Ohio and Mississippi, Andrew Ellicott arrived at Natchez with an escort of some thirty men. Named as U.S. commissioner to survey the 31° latitude, the southern boundary of the Natchez District, Ellicott immediately thrust himself into a confrontation with the now dilatory Spanish. A Quaker, somewhat condescending in his views of the frontier, Ellicott soon became entangled in quarrels both with the Spanish Governor Gayoso and some of the planters. Ellicott could hardly escape becoming controversial since he had little sympathy for either slavery or the freewheeling life of the frontiersman. As he traveled south, he kept a journal. In the first seven pages, he condemned slavery as promoting sloth, decadence, and inefficiency. He characterized some river towns as "small trifling villages, whose inhabitants are principally supported by selling liquor to the indiscreet and dissipated." [7]

The situation soon became tumultuous. Gayoso used technicalities in the treaty to delay evacuation of Fort Nogales and Natchez. Ellicott, spurning Gayoso's offer to live at his residence, took shelter in a tent under the bluffs and almost daily demanded that the Spanish leave. The planters and farmers of the region split, some favoring continued Spanish rule and others demanding immediate shift to American rule. Committees were formed, petitions circulated, and meetings held. Stephen Minor, who succeeded briefly to Gayoso's post when the latter went to New Orleans to assume the governor-generalship, reached the point of despair. "God send a speedy determination of things," he pleaded, "otherwise they will all run mad, with memorials, certificates, circular letters, etc." [8]

Even then, however, Spanish policy was once more on the verge of change. Seeing the future possibility of returning Louisiana to France, the authorities in Madrid ordered the forts in the Natchez District evacuated. Ellicott described in his journal the relinquishment he had sought since first appearing at Natchez more than a year before.

> On the 29th of March 1798 late in the evening, I was informed through a confidential channel, that the evacuation would take place the next morning, before day; in consequence of which, I rose the next morning at five o'clock, and walked to the fort, and found the last party, or rear guard just leaving it, and as the gate was left

7. Andrew Ellicott, *The Journal of Andrew Ellicott* (Philadelphia: Thomas Dobson, 1803), p. 7.

8. Arthur P. Whitaker, *The Mississippi Question, 1795–1803: A Study of Trade, Politics, and Diplomacy* (1934; reprint ed., Gloucester, Massachusetts: Peter Smith, 1962), pp. 64–65.

> open, I went in, and enjoyed from the parapet, the pleasing prospects of the gallies and boats leaving the shore and getting underway. They were out of sight of the town before daylight.[9]

Hardly did the Spanish garrison have time to reach New Orleans before the United States Congress created the Mississippi Territory.

9. Ellicott, *Journal,* p. 176.

3

The Territorial Frontier

IN May 1798 as Winthrop Sargent lay abed at Cincinnati, recovering from a severe illness, he considered his future. An officer in the Revolutionary Army and for the previous ten years secretary of the Northwest Territory, he was an ambitious man who had on May 1 observed his forty-third birthday. His real desire was to succeed to the governorship of the Northwest Territory, but he had just learned of his nomination to become the first governor of the newly established Mississippi Territory. Both his New England sense of duty and his ambitions told him to accept. It might, after all, prove to be a good steppingstone to the governorship of the Northwest. He could hardly have known on May 29, 1798, as he wrote his letter of acceptance to Secretary of State Timothy Pickering that it certainly would be a steppingstone, but into political oblivion—and within three years after his arrival at Natchez.

Winthrop Sargent was born in Gloucester, Massachusetts, on May 1, 1755, of distinguished New England lineage. He graduated from Harvard, spent a short time at sea, and in 1775 enlisted in the Revolutionary Army. By the end of the war, Sargent had risen to the rank of major. When the war ended, he signed on as a surveyor with a land company whose aim was to plant settlements in the Ohio River country. When Congress formed the Northwest Territory in 1787, Sargent became the first territorial secretary.

Ten years later he seemed to President John Adams the ideal choice to head the newly formed Mississippi Territory. Like the president, Sargent was a New England Federalist. His military experience suited a frontier territory on the far edge of American settlement that desperately needed a well-organized and trained militia. Military threats to the Mississippi Territory seemed abundant. The great Indian nations—the Chickasaws, Choctaws, and Creeks—occupied the vast heartland that separated Mississippi from the older eastern settlements. Spain still held the trans-Mississippi to the west and New Orleans to the south. Sargent's experience in the Ohio country should have proved valuable, for American frontiersmen everywhere were difficult to govern. Individualistic and naturally suspicious of too much government, the Natchez settlers were typical. Sargent recognized that, even before he set out downriver to assume his new post. Before his departure for Natchez, in June 1798, he wrote to Secretary Pickering, "From the best intelligence I have been able to procure, there prevails in the country of our destination, a refractory and turbulent spirit, with parties headed by men of perverseness and cunning—They have run wild in the recess of Government. . . . "[1] He was certainly right about that. Like most Federalists, Sargent was wary of unrestrained democracy. Like many New Englanders, he sometimes appeared condescending and stiff. A military man, he instinctively preferred command to persuasion. These were hardly traits to carry to an already contentious, egalitarian, Jeffersonian frontier.

The territory Sargent was sent to govern was laid out by act of Congress on April 7, 1798. In Congress's legal language, "all that tract of country bounded on the west by the Mississippi; on the north by a line to be drawn due east from the mouth of the Yasous [Yazoo] to the Chatahoochee river; on the east by the river Chatahoochee; and in the south by the thirty-first degree of north latitude, shall be, and hereby is constituted

[1] Dunbar Rowland, editor, *The Mississippi Territorial Archives, 1798–1803* (Nashville, Tennessee: Brandon Printing Company, 1905), p. 22.

one district, to be called the Mississippi Territory.'' [2] Congress modeled the territory on the Northwest Ordinance, stating plainly that the government and ''the rights, privileges, and advantages granted to the people'' [3] would all be precisely the same as in the older Northwest Territory. Only the provision on slavery differed. Forbidden in the northwest, that institution would be tolerated in Mississippi. Congress only forbade the foreign slave trade into the territory. Government would be strikingly undemocratic. The president, with the advice and consent of Congress, would appoint a governor, a secretary, and three judges to govern the territory. Sitting together, these five men would form a legislative council. Acting separately, they would provide the executive and judicial functions. Once the territorial population exceeded five thousand free white males, Congress could eventually allow the popular election of a lower legislative house.

During July Sargent and his military escort floated downriver toward Natchez. Sargent, not yet fully recovered from his recent illness and suffering acutely from the heat, reached Natchez in August so ill that ''for a considerable time after arrival here, my life was despaired of.'' [4] But he was soon up and about, and he needed all the strength he could muster. His problems came in hordes. A code of laws must be written and publicized, the militia organized, Indians pacified, land policy settled, Jeffersonian-leaning planters mollified, public facilities located, and counties organized. To add to Sargent's early dismay, only one of the territorial judges had yet appeared, and that one, Peter Bryan Bruin, had lived in the territory since Spanish days. The other two, Daniel Tilton of New Hampshire and William McGuire of Virginia, proved, as one historian put it, ''slow to arrive, loath to remain on the job, and eager to leave.'' [5] When John Steele

2. Clarence E. Carter, *The Territorial Papers of the United States,* 28 vols. (Washington, D.C.: Government Printing Office, 1937), 5:20.

3. Carter, *Territorial Papers,* 5:21.

4. Rowland, *Territorial Archives,* p. 301.

5. Richard A. McLemore, editor, *A History of Mississippi,* 2 vols. (Hattiesburg, Mississippi: University and College Press of Mississippi, 1973), 1:179.

of Virginia, the territorial secretary, finally arrived, he was too sick to work. Sargent seemed distraught that, even after lengthy pleas to Secretary Pickering, the official territorial seals and stationery had failed to arrive from Philadelphia. Despite the handicaps, Sargent labored on to accomplish his first two objectives, drafting a code of laws and organizing the militia.

Hardly had he begun before his enemies began to organize. His Federalism made him unpopular enough, but he must have seemed even more dictatorial to the Jeffersonian settlers, since he was frequently forced to act without the advice of the absentee judges. Many planters were hardly sympathetic. Led by the powerful family of Thomas Green and his son-in-law Cato West, an opposition faction organized and attacked Sargent for a variety of reasons. Probably they wanted office and position; certainly they, as debtors, saw it as economically disadvantageous for Sargent to side with the Federalist Natchez merchants. Perhaps they were moved by democratic-Jeffersonian idealism. Because Sargent had been appointed by Federalist President John Adams and because of the governor's imperious nature, the West-Green faction saw him as a typical Federalist—one who believed in strong central government and a strong executive—in short, a quasi-monarchy. On the other hand, Sargent's opponents, Republican followers of Thomas Jefferson, saw themselves as believers in true democracy with limited national government and local sovereignty. These views were perhaps as much expedient rationalizations as deeply held principles, for Sargent's opponents found convenient and effective allies among the Republican followers of Jefferson in the United States Congress. One feels that sometimes early Mississippians were driven by an ingrained contentiousness that often had little to do with political principle or economic status. Whatever their true motives, Sargent's enemies chose to make their fight against him on the best grounds available to them—more democracy. The West-Green group could hardly lose if they made their opposition to Sargent a fight between democracy and autocracy.

In organizing the militia and in constructing a law code, Sargent gave his opposition their first opening. Short of model codes from other states and seldom able to get a quorum of his legislative council because of the absentee judges, Sargent issued a code early in 1799. The Jeffersonian faction attacked it immediately. First, they charged, the congressional act providing for territorial government empowered the governor and the council only to *adopt* such laws from other states as fit the needs of the Mississippi Territory. Sargent, they said, had made the laws. Similarly, they objected that some penalties contained in the criminal code were draconian, providing public whipping and the pillory for many offenses. In his appointment of militia officers, they argued, Sargent commissioned only upper-crust federalists who had been closely associated with the old Spanish authorities. He should, they argued, appoint officers who were acceptable to the people in the local communities. Finally, implied in all their criticisms was the view that Sargent was an arrogant, unbending autocrat—a captive of the wealthiest planters and Natchez merchants.

The battle, which lasted from mid-1799 into early 1801, was fought through committee meetings and memorials and petitions to Congress. The Jeffersonian faction, styling themselves "a Committee regularly chosen by the Inhabitants of this Territory, for the purpose of petitioning for a redress of grievances"[6] drafted a lengthy petition to Congress outlining their position and lambasting Sargent's administration, and they appointed one of their number, Narsworthy Hunter, to carry it to Congress.

After restating the abuses and excesses of Sargent's governorship, they requested as a solution that the territory be allowed to enter the second stage of territorial government as outlined in the Northwest Ordinance. If that were done, they argued, a popularly elected territorial assembly could both curb Sargent's autocratic tendencies and calm the political tempest by allowing the same democratic rights to Mississippians that all other Americans already enjoyed. With a presidentially appointed governor and judges in whom all the functions of government were vested, they reminded Congress, citizens of the Missis-

6. Carter, *Territorial Papers,* 5:78.

sippi Territory did not enjoy the fundamental rights of other Americans. Their course, they professed, was the same as that of the American Revolutionary patriots. They had, they proclaimed, "bled in the cause of America" during the Revolution against "the usurped power of Britain, to compel Americans to obey laws and pay taxes which had not their own consent." The Northwest Ordinance, they charged, subverted that very hard-won principle of representative government. "The executive, legislative, and Judicial authorities so carefully separated and limited by the constitution of the Elder states" were in the Mississippi Territory, they continued, "mingled together in the hands of three or four individuals." [7]

Sargent defended his actions vigorously in letters to Secretary Pickering and President Adams. He noted that neither in population, wealth, nor political sophistication was the territory ready for the second stage of territorial government. To the charge that he had made arbitrary and unconstitutional laws, he pleaded an absence in the territory of law books that could be used as models. He answered the charge that he was arrogant, arbitrary, and willing to associate only with the rich and powerful by admitting that he was not "over anxious of popularity." However, he continued, "No man . . . more ardently desires the approbation of the Wise and the Good than myself, but I shall never be so far degraded, as to become the Machine of the Multitude." [8]

The result could hardly be in doubt. The year 1800 brought the election of Thomas Jefferson to the presidency. Even earlier, Congress on May 10, 1800, ordered the election of a territorial assembly for the Mississippi Territory. Refusing even then to concede defeat, Sargent gathered the signatures of his supporters on a petition asking Congress to reverse the decision. The effort was fruitless. Governor Sargent's public career was almost at an end. Mississippi voters returned a solid slate of Sargent's opponents to the new legislature. One of Thomas Jefferson's first decisions upon assuming the presidency was to

7. Carter, *Territorial Papers,* 5:81.

8. Rowland, *Territorial Archives,* p. 315.

remove Winthrop Sargent and replace him with the young, politically more astute William Charles Cole Claiborne. Sargent, after a brief visit to his native Massachusetts, returned to Natchez and lived the quiet life of a planter until his death in New Orleans in 1820.

W. C. C. Claiborne, vigorous at the age of twenty-six, a protégé of Jefferson and a native of Virginia, suited the quarrelsome and touchy democrats of the Mississippi Territory somewhat better. His career had been meteoric. Thrown on his own resources at age fifteen because of a bankrupt father, Claiborne became a copy boy for Congress. At the age of eighteen, after three months' preparation in law, he gained admission to the Virginia bar. Emigrating to Tennessee, at age twenty-one he served in that state's first constitutional convention. At age twenty-two, he was appointed to the Tennessee Supreme Court, only to resign within the year to run successfully for Congress. He took his seat at age twenty-three, in contravention of the constitutional age limit of twenty-five for congressmen. He was serving his second term there when his appointment as governor of the Mississippi Territory came from his friend Thomas Jefferson. Claiborne already knew something of the Mississippi Territory and its problems. Recently he had sat on the committee that heard the West-Green petitions against Sargent, and in that confrontation he sided with Sargent's opponents.

Claiborne was in Nashville, Tennessee, when he received Jefferson's commission appointing him governor of the Mississippi Territory. In the middle of September 1801, he wrote to Secretary of State James Madison that he would set out for Natchez during the first week of October. He noted reports from the territory that led him to believe that all was tranquil there and that the recent political turmoil had completely subsided. Because of low water in the rivers, it took Claiborne six weeks to make the journey from Nashville to Natchez. Upon his arrival on November 23, 1801, affairs did, indeed, seem more calm. Partisanship still existed, and Claiborne recognized it. He did not, like Sargent, allow factionalism to dominate his activities. He passed off the partisan backbiting as normal activities among a bumptious and impetuous people. The approaching legislative elections, he wrote to James Madison in March 1802, disturbed "the quietude of this little society." Campaigning, he continued, was "infinitely more rancorous than any I have ever witnessed in our Mother States." He predicted politics would probably "rage with unabated fury, until the elections are over" [9] and then return to normal. He voiced much more concern over two other evils. While he recognized the loyalty and patriotism of the majority, "to my great mortification there are persons here . . . favorable to Monarchy, and inimical to every Government that recognizes the Rights of Man." [10] Too, he lamented the growing slave population. If the number of slaves continued to increase, he predicted, the institution would "in all probability, (sooner or later) prove a source of much distress," and if cotton continued to expand, "this Territory must soon be overrun, by the most *abandoned of that unfortunate race*." [11]

Claiborne recognized that, ultimately, extreme partisanship could only be quelled by attacking the real problems of the territory, and they were legion. Most important among them were those that had foiled Sargent—organization of an effective militia, pacification of the Indians, organization of the judiciary, a new code of laws to replace the now discredited Sargent's Code, and, perhaps most vexing of all, the amicable settlement of conflicting and overlapping land grants. Claiborne realized, as Sargent had not, that the territorial legislature was an asset, not a liability. If nothing else, it served as a handy lightning rod to keep political fire from centering entirely on the governor.

Slowly, order began to emerge. Claiborne, though perhaps naive in assuming that the factional fighting had ended, worked hard. His personality suited the frontier. Where Sargent was aloof, Claiborne was familiar. Where Sargent was often stiff-necked, Claiborne was almost too pliable and accommodating. Most important of all, as a Jeffersonian, Claiborne was deeply committed to republican ideals and to frontier democracy. One

9. Dunbar Rowland, editor, *Official Letterbooks of W. C. C. Claiborne*, 6 vols. (Jackson, Mississippi: State Department of Archives and History, 1917), 1:54.

10. Rowland, *Official Letterbooks*, 1:47.

11. Rowland, *Official Letterbooks*, 1:39.

by one, the problems that afflicted the territory began to be solved.

To make his position plain, Claiborne immediately removed the capital from Federalist-merchant-dominated Natchez to Washington, a little village six miles to the north. The problem of judicial absenteeism, so debilitating to Sargent, came under control. Judge Daniel Tilton left the territory on a trip to Europe without obtaining permission. In his place, Jefferson chose a resident of the territory, David Ker. Seth Lewis resigned, to be replaced by Judge Thomas Rodney, a Jefferson supporter from Delaware. Not only did the new judges stay on the job, but they knew something of the law, a field in which their predecessors had been deficient.

Sargent had been adamant on the governor's right to appoint militia officers. The result was that many citizens boycotted the periodic musters, and when Claiborne assumed office, that essential military arm was in utter disarray. Claiborne, undoubtedly to the horror of such old soldiers as Sargent, proposed "that the privates composing the different Military Companies shall nominate (by election) such Characters as they would wish me to Commission . . . and my determination is to appoint every *person* so recommended, unless there should exist some *good* objection either to his Public or Private Character." [12]

Claiborne suited the avaricious frontiersmen, too, in his views of the Indians who occupied the vast interior domain and the Spanish who controlled East and West Florida to the south. He favored United States expansion into those lands. On one occasion, when the Spanish in 1802 closed the port of New Orleans to American goods, he favored a military expedition to wrest New Orleans from Spain's control. He assured Secretary of State Madison that, with six hundred militiamen, he could take possession of the city, "provided there should be only Spanish troops to defend the place." [13]

It was, in fact, this problem which in December 1803 sepa-

12. Rowland, *Official Letterbooks,* 1:103.
13. Rowland, *Official Letterbooks,* 1:253.

rated Claiborne from the Mississippi Territory. After Spain returned Louisiana to France in 1803, France promptly sold New Orleans and the vast interior lands of Louisiana to the United States; Jefferson ordered Claiborne to New Orleans to accept the newly purchased domain. Although initially this assignment was only an additional duty for Claiborne, he never returned to Mississippi. Appointed as the first governor of the Orleans Territory, then later elected state governor and senator from Louisiana, Claiborne's later career, until his untimely death at age forty-two, is identified with that state.

When, in September of 1804, Claiborne announced that he would not return to Mississippi, the territory found itself once again entangled in a political brawl. Cato West, Claiborne's secretary and leader of the Green faction that had unseated Sargent, acted as governor from Claiborne's departure in late 1803 until mid-1806. West wanted the governorship desperately. When Jefferson instead appointed as governor Robert Williams, land commissioner for the territory west of the Pearl River, West was irate. In a fit of petulance, he carried off the official papers of the territory to his home. Only when the legislature threatened to fine him did he return them.

Williams's assumption of the governorship hardly ended the bickering. Mistakenly assuming that all was calm, Williams left in May 1806 to visit his native North Carolina. He left his new secretary, Cowles Mead, in charge. At that moment the temporary calm broke. On January 19, 1807, former Vice-President Aaron Burr arrived north of Natchez at Bruinsburg, leading several boatloads of adventurers.

Burr's purpose is not to this day known. Much evidence implicates both Burr and General James Wilkinson in a plot to capture New Orleans and use it as a base from which to foster revolution among the settlements of the Mississippi and Ohio valleys, to bring about their secession from the United States, and to establish a great western empire. Others thought Burr intended to wrest Texas and Mexico from Spain. Considering Burr's personality, it is hardly credible that he was not up to something inimical to the interests of the United States. President Jefferson, who already suspected something of Burr's probable plans, had already warned Governor Robert Williams of the Mississippi Territory and Governor W. C. C. Claiborne of the Orleans Territory to be on guard.

Burr's plans collapsed entirely upon his arrival in the Mississippi Territory. Cowles Mead, acting as governor in the absence of Williams, received the conspirator's surrender at Burr's rendezvous point on the plantation of Judge Peter Bryan Bruin. Burr had already learned that General Wilkinson, United States military commander in the west and his erstwhile fellow plotter, had deserted his cause and had ordered Burr's arrest. Burr chose instead to place himself in the hands of the Mississippi authorities for trial. Convinced that if Burr had any conspiratorial designs, they were against Spanish Mexico, the territorial supreme court failed to bring Burr to trial and refused even to indict him. Arrested north of Mobile, as he made his way toward Spanish Pensacola, Burr was transported to Richmond, Virginia, tried and acquitted in one of the most sensational trials in American history.

Burr's temporary sojourn in the Mississippi Territory proved two things. First, factionalism was far from dead. The Jeffersonians were discomfited, for they seriously mishandled the Burr trial, allowing him to slip through their fingers. The old Sargent-Federalist group enjoyed the embarrassment of their Jeffersonian enemies immensely. Furthermore, Burr had friends in Mississippi, notably Bruin and Stephen Minor, both of whom had been officials under the old Spanish regime. Whether they knew all of Burr's designs is uncertain, yet his very presence shook the territory and fostered fears of secession and disloyalty. Burr's brief appearance proved that the Mississippi Territory was on the far edge of American control, tied to the older states only by the thread of a common ethnic background. That tenuous connection could easily be broken by economic or political self-interest.

After 1807 political power passed to a new and younger coalition of politically ambitious men. Cowles Mead, who had been removed from office by Jefferson in the aftermath of the Burr affair, found allies in George Poindexter, an irascible, office-hungry lawyer and former territorial attorney general, and

Ferdinand L. Claiborne, Governor Claiborne's brother, who had been removed as head of the militia by Williams. By capturing the legislature and flaying Williams in the press, they forced the governor's retirement in 1809. When Williams officially relinquished the office on March 3, 1809, Jefferson already had offered the post to David Holmes of Virginia.

After 1809, when David Holmes assumed the governorship, political peace settled over the Mississippi Territory. For a variety of reasons, the factional fighting of previous years subsided. If, after 1809, the political differences did not dissipate entirely, Mississippians at least fought over more substantial issues than in past years. In the first place, Holmes's personality—pleasant, accommodating, and deliberate—served to calm tensions. The problems with Britain, which finally erupted into war in 1812, diverted energy from the personal ambitions and clashes that had earlier characterized territorial politics. The uprising by the Creek Indians in the eastern part of the territory in 1813–1814 presented Mississippians with their first great Indian war since French times. Most important of all, however, after 1809 the territory developed real political differences, based largely on an east-west sectionalism that in turn was grounded in distinct divergences in economic interests, politics, ideals, and life style.

At the time Congress created the Mississippi Territory in 1798, the Natchez District overshadowed the smaller, poorer, less populated, and more isolated settlements along the Tombigbee and Alabama rivers north of Mobile Bay. By the time the War of 1812 was under way, the river counties of Adams, Jefferson, Claiborne, and Wilkinson faced submergence in a tide of territorial expansion that favored those settlements east of the Pearl River. Both in land area and in population the territory expanded explosively.

By the end of the war in 1815, the settlements east of the Pearl rivaled the river counties in population, if not in wealth and sophistication. These eastern settlements had not always weighed heavily in territorial affairs. Upon taking possession of the eastern settlements along the Tombigbee River in 1799, the American representative reported only 131 men capable of militia duty. The leading citizen of the eastern country, according to another report, was "Spanish when sober, violently American when drunk." [14] In answer to a series of questions posed by President Jefferson about the settlements east of the Pearl River, Ephraim Kirby, recently appointed land commissioner, wrote that the population was sparse, that the lands in the river bottoms of the Tombigbee and Mobile rivers were extremely productive, but that the pine barrens between the Pearl and the Tombigbee could never support a dense population. Of the settlers already there, he was contemptuous:

> The section of the United States had long afforded an assylum [*sic*] to those who prefer voluntary exile to the punishments ordained by law for heinous offences.—The present inhabitants (with few exceptions) are illiterate, wild and savage, of depraved morals, unworthy of public confidence or private esteem; litigious, disunited, and knowing each other, universally distrustful of each other. The magistrates without dignity, respect, probity, influence or authority.—The administration of justice, imbecile and corrupt. The militia without discipline or competent officers.[15]

The smallest group and, according to Kirby, the only respectable element was composed of the descendants of the French. Another group from the Carolinas and Georgia wandered into these eastern lands during the American Revolution—Tories who "not only hate the American government, but having long lived without any restraint . . . are now hostile to all law and every government." Finally, Kirby noted, a third class, also mostly from Georgia and the Carolinas who had come after 1798, was composed of "mostly poor people who have come hither to avoid the demands of creditors, or to gain a precarious subsistence in the wilderness." [16]

One other pocket of settlement developed early in the territorial period in the lands that lay in the bend of the Tennessee River near the Tennessee line. Like the Tombigbee settlements, this outpost was settled sparsely, at first, from Tennessee,

14. William B. Hamilton, "American Beginnings in the Old South-West: The Mississippi Phase" (Ph.D. dissertation, Duke University, 1937), p. 174.
15. Carter, *Territorial Papers,* 1:323–324.
16. Carter, *Territorial Papers,* 1:324.

Virginia, and the Carolinas. Also like the Tombigbee area, the bend of the Tennessee held great promise for future growth.

Population in the territory, especially after the Creek War ended in 1815, zoomed upward, and the lands east of the Pearl drew a disproportionate share of these new immigrants. In 1798 no more than 5,000 people inhabited the territory, and the majority of those resided in the Old Natchez District. By 1800 there were 7,600. By 1810 the population had almost quintupled, to 31,306. By 1820, the first census after statehood, 75,448 persons lived in Mississippi, and that figure excluded the eastern area, which, by then, had become the state of Alabama. Even by 1810, of the 31,306 inhabitants in the territory, slightly more than 10,000 lived in the settlements east of the Pearl. Moreover, slaves in the population of the river counties exceeded 50 percent, while only about one-third of the population in the eastern counties was slave. Hence, in white population, the east already rivaled the west.

Therefore, by the end of the territorial period, real sectionalism developed. The river counties—already heavily dependent on slavery and cotton, conservative in political and economic views, and on the way to developing a gentry—faced the rising influence of the eastern sections. The easterners depended less on slavery and cotton and more on small subsistence farming and herding. More egalitarian than aristocratic, they distrusted the wealth and growing sophistication of Natchez. In short, the territorial period gave birth to a rough east-west sectionalism that in some respects pervades Mississippi history and persists into the present—a sectionalism that divided economic classes, political ideals, and social views. Even by 1803 the sectional tension was great enough to produce a request for separations from the territory by the eastern settlements. Separated as the easterners were by "a howling wilderness with its usual inhabitants of savages and beasts of prey" and "composed of people different in their manners and customs, different in their interests," they explained, "nature appears never to have designed the two countries to be under the same government." [17]

17. Carter, *Territorial Papers,* 1:290.

If the territory exploded in population during the period from 1798 to 1817, it more than doubled in land area, so that, by 1817, before Congress divided it, the Mississippi Territory included everything presently within the boundaries of Mississippi and Alabama. Originally, the territorial boundaries were the Mississippi on the west and the Chattahoochee on the east, 31° latitude on the south and 32°28′ on the north. The first great addition came in 1804, when Congress added to the territory all lands north of 32°28′ up to the Tennessee line. Most of that area remained closed to settlement until well after statehood, when it was ceded to the United States by the Choctaws and Chickasaws. Two important Indian cessions, however, were negotiated in the territorial period. In 1805 the Choctaws relinquished a large tract in the Piney Woods that served to link the Tombigbee settlements to the river counties. In 1816 the Chickasaws handed over a smaller tract east of the Tombigbee River in the northern part of the territory.

Another great addition had already come in 1813. The United States maintained before 1810 that the coastal lands below 31°, between the Mississippi and the Perdido rivers, had been a part of the Louisiana Purchase. Yet Spain continued to occupy West Florida. In 1810 American settlers in that portion of West Florida between the Mississippi and the Pearl rose in revolt against continued Spanish rule. Spurred on by inhabitants of the Mississippi Territory to the north, the settlers declared their new state the Republic of West Florida and asked for annexation by the United States. President Madison promptly complied, announcing the annexation of West Florida all the way to the Perdido. To the chagrin of Mississippians, Congress in 1812 added the lands between the Mississippi and the Pearl to Louisiana. In 1813, however, that portion of West Florida from the Pearl to the Perdido was added to the Mississippi Territory. With that, the territory reached its greatest extent, containing all lands presently within the bounds of Mississippi and Alabama. These additions tended to strengthen the eastern settlements against the older and hitherto dominant Natchez area.

The sectional cleavage between east and west was spurred forward in the territorial period by the rapid emergence of two economic and social worlds. The now cotton-crazed western river counties increasingly transformed their embryonic plantation system from provincial Spanish days into a cotton-slave-plantation economy that in the counties around Natchez eventually produced a baronial mentality almost royal in its grandiose trappings. The east meanwhile remained a land of small farmers more accustomed to corn and cattle than cotton, family labor than slave, and dogtrot log cabins than mansions. Both worlds were overwhelmingly agricultural. No manufacturing establishments of consequence existed, and trade was simple—exportation to Europe and the eastern states of staple agricultural commodities and the importation of luxuries and even, sometimes, the necessities of life.

One historian has set 1800 as the date when the Natchez area began to pass from frontier rudeness into civilization. However debatable that date may be, it cannot be doubted that the territorial period produced in the river counties one of the first outposts of a great plantation society in the Southwest. Though the great mansions awaited a later time, by 1817 cotton was ubiquitous in the western counties. The lands produced abundantly, and the price was high. Planters cultivated their profits as assiduously as they cultivated cotton, plowing back profits into more land to raise more cotton to buy more slaves. Certainly many became wealthy. A New England farmer earned by hard labor perhaps $700 in a year. A Natchez planter with the same acreage could earn ten times more. His profits in good years approached 30 percent on his investment. On five hundred acres of cultivable land, with the work of fifty slaves, the typical planter grew perhaps two hundred acres of cotton, on which he produced perhaps a hundred bales of four hundred pounds each. At 20¢ per pound, his cotton crop brought $8,000. His investment in land, slaves, and implements totaled perhaps $35,000. In addition, he turned profits on the sale of excess corn and livestock. The successful cotton planter found himself on the high road to wealth.

Agents in New Orleans or Liverpool served as the planters' liaison with the world. They sold the planters' cotton and contracted in turn for the Madeira, china, furniture, and fine clothing required by the planters' family. It was a system that promoted a style of life and a view of affairs unusual on the American continent. In democratic America, the Natchez planter was an anomaly. On the far reaches of backwoods America, around a small river town, there began to develop a class that found its counterparts more in the English gentry, the Prussian Junkers, or the Russian boyars than among the Jeffersonian agrarians who were the American ideal.

Yet it has been too easy for historians to popularize the cotton-slave-plantation South as typified by the great baronial planters of Natchez. They represented a phenomenon still romanticized in novels and motion pictures. Because they left records, because they entertained the foreign writers, because they are unique in American history, the Natchez planters are more vivid in today's history and fiction books than in their own time. In the Mississippi Territory, the planter was the exception. The vast majority of Mississippians were farmers, not planters.

East of the Pearl River, in the piney woods, planters could hardly be found. Here lived farmers, Scotch-Irish from the hills of the Carolinas, and they did not farm cotton, nor own slaves, nor import china, nor drink Madeira. Nonetheless, they were hardly poor whites. They grew corn for their and their livestock's subsistence, and they planted vegetables. But their staple crop was livestock—cattle and hogs, which they allowed to wander in the pine woods and which they drove to market in Mobile and New Orleans once a year. They shunned the pretensions of the Natchez planter, and they left few detailed records, for their life was pastoral, independent, egalitarian, and proud. With their greater numbers they, more than the Natchez barons, molded Mississippi.

Territorial Mississippians hardly led a genteel life. Luxuries were common only among the planters, travel was arduous and dangerous, violence quick to erupt, health precarious, and education rudimentary or lacking altogether. Few Mississippians in 1817 were natives. Most had journeyed into the territory by various routes over the previous decade. The older states of the South—Virginia, the Carolinas, Georgia, and Tennessee—furnished more Mississippi settlers than any other region. Slavery had not yet become a great divisive national issue, and during the years of the territory both New Englanders and natives of the Middle Atlantic states came in significant numbers. All were on the make, coming to a country of great opportunity with few restraints and fewer refinements. Society was fluid, and life was hazardous.

Violence cut some down suddenly and senselessly. One such episode, as told years later by a participant, arose, he said, "from some cause which I do not recollect at this time." Though it happened at Natchez in 1827, it as easily could have occurred at Dodge City in 1870. Both duelists, Dr. Thomas H. Maddox and Samuel L. Wells, survived, but the bloodshed among their attending parties was quick and complete. As Maddox remembered,

> Two rounds were fired without effect, and the affair was then settled by Mr. S. L. Wells withdrawing all offensive language. We shook hands, and were proceeding to my friends . . . when Gen. Cuney, James Bowie, and Jeff. Wells came running down on us; Gen. Cuney saying to Col. Crain that this was a good time to settle their difficulties, he Cuney, and James Bowie drawing their pistols. Col. Crain . . . shot the one whom he conceived to be "Major General" [Cuney] of the party through the breast . . . Col. Crain, after shooting at Bowie, who had also shot at him, wheeled around and . . . he and Cuney fired simultaneously at each other, when Cuney fell, mortally wounded, and then Col. Crain, with an empty pistol in his hand, turned to meet James Bowie . . . I, at that time, had a pistol pointed at me . . . and, being totally unarmed myself, I ran to the edge of the woods . . . to get my shot gun; and on returning . . . I found my friend, Maj. Wright, dead, and Gen. Cuney dying from excessive hemorrhage, Bowie badly wounded, and Alfred Blanchard slightly wounded.[18]

If dueling—or perhaps *gunfighting* is a better term—was responsible for some untimely departures from this life, the ravages of fever carried away far more. Because of the long, hot summers, the nearness to the tropics, and the multitudinous

18. Thomas H. Maddox Papers, no. 1753, Southern Historical Collection, University of North Carolina Library, Chapel Hill, N.C.

mosquitoes, Mississippi early earned a grim reputation as a most unhealthful place. Physicians were scarce and inclined to leave practice as soon as they could stake themselves to a cotton plantation. Had they been as numerous as the mosquitoes, however, they could not have protected the population from the "intermittent" or "bilious" fevers, which rose, they thought, from the "miasmas" of the swamps. The settlers, of course, suffered from the mosquito-borne diseases of malaria and yellow fever. In bad years of the fever, the death rate approached 10 percent. Common treatments called for purging, opium, and bloodletting. Smallpox was occasional, and respiratory ailments carried settlers off in droves. It is little wonder that Mississippians were obsessed with their health. Hardly anyone wrote a letter in which he did not comment on the state of his own health and inquire about that of his addressee. At Natchez the only hospital barely functioned for lack of funds.

Formal education in the territory was scarcely available and public education was nonexistent. A few wealthy planters hired tutors or sent their children to Philadelphia or Virginia or Europe. However, because of the scattered nature of settlement, most inhabitants depended on what rudiments could be taught at home. Others entrusted their children to itinerant preacher-teachers or to young northerners whose real ambition was to own a cotton plantation or to gain admission to the bar.

The grandest educational dream, which it largely remained, was Jefferson College. Governor Claiborne first suggested the college in 1802, and the territorial legislature issued a charter for the college in the same year. But because of the lack of money and prolonged factional squabbling over its location, the college did not accept students for almost a decade. Located finally at Washington, Jefferson College never fulfilled its promise. Plagued by niggardly support, the college depended almost entirely on fees and donations. These were insufficient. Those who could afford to pay left the territory for their education. Those who could not afford education brought their knowledge with them when they came to Mississippi or they went without.

Many brought their education in with them. Bright young New Englanders, educated in that region's already renowned colleges, arrived to make their fortunes. The liveliest profession in Mississippi, and a quick way to fame and fortune, was the bar. Admission usually proved easy—one appeared before a sympathetic judge and proved through examination that he had "read" the law. If successful, he hung out a shingle to attract some unsuspecting client. Because of the many conflicting land claims and the Mississippi frontiersman's appetite for lawsuits, business generally proved brisk. Legal talent was uneven. Territorial Judge Thomas Rodney was a legal scholar. Territorial Judge Peter Bryan Bruin was devoid of legal training and prone to strong drink. The aim of many lawyers, like their medical counterparts, was a cotton plantation; hence many of the ablest members of the bar became, eventually, planter-attorney-politicians.

Territorial Mississippi proved to be a fertile ground for evangelical preachers. If one believes contemporary accounts of morality, Methodist and Baptist moral fervor was nowhere more needed, and nowhere west of China were there more souls in need of saving. Natchez-under-the-Hill was renowned throughout the Mississippi valley for its rowdiness and vice. One early visitor counted thirteen bawdy houses lining the river front. Remarkably, for a state later known for the intensity of its Baptist and Methodist fundamentalism, one finds little mention in the territory of formally oganized churches. Before 1798 the Spanish authorities allowed only Roman Catholic services to be observed publicly. After 1798, with the Spanish gone, the Roman Catholic church shrank into insignificance. Neither is there any record of Anglican worship in the territory. A number of Congregationalists entered the territory during the British period, when the Reverend Samuel Swayze led a group of settlers from New Jersey into the Cole's Creek area north of Natchez. The Presbyterians began to organize through a missionary effort in 1800. In the backwoods, the fields lay open to itinerant Baptist and Methodist preachers who held camp meetings and railed against the sin and vice of Natchez (even then any city was a place of evil). Yet they left few organized churches behind. Bringing religion to the Mississippi Territory was an uphill fight. The backwoods sections were lawless and isolated, while the river counties, busily accumulating the fruits of this world, paid little attention to preparation for the next.

By 1817 Natchez had already begun to take on pretensions. But along with the encasement of one-room log cabins with columned additions and the daily ease brought by increasing wealth came some troubling questions. By the time of statehood in 1817, the slave population of the four oldest river counties was well beyond 50 percent, and for the slaveholder his chattels posed a moral and intellectual dilemma. As the numbers of blacks continued to grow, fear of insurrection plagued the planter. Despite the growing profitability of the institution, politicians and planters could voice reservations about slavery. As Charles S. Sydnor, the most famous historian of Mississippi slavery, put it, in the territorial period Mississippians "occasionally admitted the evils of slavery and almost never attempted to justify it." [19]

Perhaps George Poindexter, a leading planter-politician-lawyer, expressed the slaveholder's dilemma best in 1818. Slavery, he said, was not for Mississippians "a matter of choice. . . . We found them here, and we are obliged to maintain and employ them. It would be a blessing could we get rid of them; but the wisest and best men among us have not been able to devise a plan for doing it." [20] The Mississippi Supreme Court in the same year wrote, "Slavery is condemned by reason and the laws of nature. It exists and can only exist, through municipal regulations." [21] Slavery was an evil, the position seemed to be, but the unknown alternative of a large free-black population was worse. Of course the profit that slaves brought and the investment they represented prevented any real efforts at emancipation. Yet even these intellectual doubts about the institution would be impossible after 1840. What most slaves thought on the matter can only be guessed.

The material conditions of Mississippi slaves were probably little different from those of slaves elsewhere. Harsh slave laws

19. Charles S. Sydnor, *Slavery in Mississippi* (New York: D. Appleton-Century Company, 1933), p. 245.

20. Sydnor, *Slavery in Mississippi*, p. 239.

21. Sydnor, *Slavery in Mississippi*, p. 239.

forbade to slaves weapons, liquor, private property, and trade and placed upon them all manner of other restrictions. Yet two things are apparent. First, these restrictions were designed for the social control of a subject population, not for the purposes of labor. Second, the rigid regulations were only laxly enforced, except in times of rumored insurrections. Accounts of the time are filled with laments that slaves, especially around Natchez, were not kept under closer control. Slaves clogged the town on weekends, selling and trading vegetables. Often they came and went freely, despite the requirement for passes; they came to town to drink and hire themselves out, both strictly forbidden; and they even on occasion ran and patronized saloons.

Apparently, too, the Mississippi planter of territorial days was not as fearful of miscegenation as his descendants would later be. Numerous instances of cohabitation were openly admitted. The mulatto children of these unions formed the core of Mississippi's free Negro population. In fact, it had become somewhat fashionable by the time of statehood to free slaves by last will and testament and to leave a bequest to remove them to free territory or to Liberia.

If this picture of territorial slavery seems benevolent, assuredly white Mississippians changed their views later. In the 1830s, attitudes changed, and slavery ceased in Mississippi minds to be a necessary evil and became instead a positive good—an institution whites criticized only on peril of ostracism.

Talk of the territory's admission to the Union began as early as 1812. The War of 1812 and the uprising by the Creek Indians that threatened the eastern settlements in 1813 intervened to postpone any serious drive for statehood. By 1815, however, the war was over and the Creek uprising quelled. Louisiana gained admission to the Union in 1812, and by 1815 a serious drive dedicated to statehood began both in Mississippi and Washington. Still, however, serious problems blocked the path. Some in the national capital believed that the territory was too large to form one state, and they insisted on the division of the territory. Though slavery was not yet a divisive national issue, some welcomed division, since it would eventually create two slave states from one territory. The chief problem remained the east-west sectionalism that had sprung up in the years since 1798. Immigration after the end of the War of 1812 favored the eastern settlements, and although they had supported division earlier, when they were at the mercy of the richer, more populous river counties, now they saw prospects of dominating any state that encompassed the entire territory. Conversely, the river counties, long opposed to division, were by 1815 increasingly fearful that without division their interests would be overwhelmed by the backwoods.

In 1815 the maneuvering began in earnest. The idea of splitting the territory was not new. In 1811 George Poindexter, the territorial delegate to Congress, attempted to gain approval for a north-south division. His unsuccessful proposal would have added all of West Florida to Mississippi and divided the territory at the old 32°28′ line, admitting the southern half as a state.

In 1815 a convention dominated by the eastern counties met on the Pearl River and adopted a petition to Congress calling for the admission of the entire territory as one state. They sent Judge Harry Toulmin to Washington to lobby for their cause. Mississippi's territorial delegate to Congress was William Lattimore who, as a westerner, favored division. He introduced a counterproposal calling upon Congress to allow the western counties of the Mississippi Territory to write a constitution, form a government, and enter the Union.

By 1816 it was apparent to the easterners that Congress would insist upon division, but along what line? The easterners favored the Pearl River as the dividing line. Some westerners wanted a line far enough east to include Mobile in the new state. Lattimore and the easterners finally agreed upon a line beginning west of Mobile that ran due north from the Gulf to the northwestern corner of Washington County (Alabama) and from there slightly northeast to the mouth of Bear Creek on the Tennessee River. Thus Mobile was excluded, but the coastal settlements on the Pascagoula, at Biloxi Bay, and on Bay Saint Louis would be included in the new state. All was settled, if not amicably, at least permanently. On March 1, 1817, President Madison signed legislation confirming that boundary and allowing the western counties to write a constitution and form a government. The eastern settlements immediately formed the Alabama Territory.

Now that the road was cleared, the citizens wasted little time. Forty-eight delegates from fourteen counties met in July at the Methodist Church in the village of Washington outside Natchez to write a constitution. They were men of wealth and influence. Territorial Governor David Holmes presided, and three former territorial secretaries, two former delegates to Congress, and three former territorial judges sat in the convention. So did the men who would become Mississippi's first four state governors. Only one was a native of the territory. Most, like the voters they represented, had been born and reared in the older states of the South. Because after division of the territory the counties west of the Pearl contained two-thirds of the population of the proposed state, they dominated the convention. Half of the forty-eight delegates came from the five river counties of Warren, Claiborne, Jefferson, Adams, and Wilkinson. Another eight came from the adjacent counties of Franklin and Amite. Not unexpectedly, the constitution that they hammered out in six weeks of summer heat embodied conservative republican principles. For a western state, much of which was still frontier, the Constitution of 1817 was amazingly conservative.

The issue of sectionalism was not dead. A sizable minority of the delegates still grumbled about the division of the territory. At best they hoped to postpose statehood and force Congress to re-examine the issue. At least, they hoped to force removal of the dividing line farther to the east so that Mobile and the settlements along the Tombigbee could be included in the new state. George Poindexter moved to postpone the convention until March 15, 1818. In the meantime, he hoped Congress would relent. The motion failed, with only fourteen delegates voting for postponement. The same question failed later in the convention on a tie vote.

Sectionalism, not unexpectedly, also surfaced on several other issues. Perhaps the most important was apportionment. The heavily slave-populated river counties wished their slaves to be included for representation in the legislature. The eastern sections wished representation to be based on white population.

Finally, the delegates compromised, and the constitution provided that representation in the lower house would be based on white population, with every county to have at least one representative. Representation was based on white taxable inhabitants, thus favoring the wealthier river counties that had a higher proportion of property owners than the newer counties east of the Pearl. Because of parochial interests the convention never agreed on a state capital. The Adams County representatives wanted Natchez as the permanent seat of government, but on that issue Adams Countians could not count even on their allies from the other river counties. The constitution finally provided that the first meeting of the general assembly would be at Natchez. Thereafter, the legislature itself would choose a seat of government.

The constitution gave the franchise to white male taxpayers or members of the militia. Property qualifications were prescribed for holding office. Representatives must own 150 acres or real estate worth $500; senators, 300 acres or $1000; and the governor, 600 acres or $2000. One-year terms were prescribed for representatives, three-year terms for senators, and two-year terms for governors. Yet, in true frontier fashion, the constitution provided for a weak executive and a strong legislature. Apparently, the delegates fully trusted neither the governor nor the people, for the appointment of many state officials—the secretary of state, treasurer, auditor, and all judges—was vested in the general assembly. Judges were given tenure for good behavior or until age sixty-five. Oddly, belief in a supreme being was made mandatory for officeholding, but ministers were ineligible.

The article on slavery reflected territorial ambivalence toward that institution. It forbade the legislature the power to emancipate slaves without the owner's consent, except when a slave provided distinguished service to the state. Even then the state was required to provide compensation. The article affirmed the right of immigrants to bring their slaves with them but empowered the general assembly to forbid the bringing of slaves into the state as merchandise, a right that body chose not to exercise. It also required owners to treat their slaves humanely, not injure them, and to provide for them the essentials of life. The state could forcibly sell the slaves of owners who failed in their responsibilities. It is, in fact, remarkable that a system of such social and economic importance should be treated in the Constitution of 1817 so briefly.

The delegates finished their work on August 15, 1817. They chose not to submit the finished document to the voters for ratification. Hardly had the constitution been completed before many Mississippians, especially the ever-more-numerous backwoodsmen, began to criticize it as undemocratic. It was destined to endure only for fifteen years before being replaced by a new instrument of government, one that was an almost perfect statement of Jacksonian Democracy. Congress and the president, however, approved, and the voters chose legislators, a governor, and a congressional representative. The legislature, in turn, chose two United States senators, and on December 10, 1817, Mississippi became the nation's twentieth state.

4

A Different Road

MISSISSIPPI'S history before statehood parallels the American frontier experience. The institutions, aspirations, and ideals of her people sprang from American values. Mississippians were in the American tradition: Protestant, acquisitive, democratic, individualistic, and jealous of their rights. On the surface appeared differences—distinctive historical marks that seemed to set Mississippi apart even then. Certainly Mississippi was first settled by the French, not the English, and she was ruled for a time by the Spanish; yet those powers left few legacies. After 1770 the population of Mississippi was as British as that of the former English colonies. Even slavery as a labor and social system did not set Mississippi apart, for until the early nineteenth century slavery was not peculiarly Southern, but an institution condoned by Americans, albeit with some moral and intellectual doubts, and practiced by almost all nations of the western world. Mississippi planters, though they may have profited from slavery more than many others, harbored as many reservations of conscience and mind about it as most other Americans. The emergence of the Natchez plantation baronies was unique in America. Yet the Natchez nabobs hardly dominated Mississippi, either in numbers or influence—before statehood or after. Mississippians held to their democratic faith as fiercely as any other Americans.

Then what set Mississippians on a different road, a road that led not only to secession and civil war but, afterwards, to a peculiarity and insularity remarkable for its persistence? The events that transformed Mississippi's institutions began in 1820.

Doak's Stand was a flat, open field in the fertile lands north of present-day Canton. There, in early October 1820, led by their chiefs Pushmataha, Puckshunubbee, and Mushulatubbee, several hundred Choctaw Indians began gathering, to be plied for three weeks with twenty thousand dollars' worth of beef, corn, and liquor. They were the guests of the United States government. Government representatives had earlier selected the site and planned the party. Leaders for the event were two westerners of great distinction who personified not only the aspirations of the southwestern frontiersmen, but also themselves embodied the ideals of frontier success. They were Generals Andrew Jackson and Thomas Hinds, old Indian fighters from the Creek War and heroes of the Battle of New Orleans. Despite the carnival surroundings, neither whites nor Indians suffered any illusions about the real purpose of their gathering. Both groups knew that Jackson intended to lull the Indians, through bribery and drink, or if required, to overawe them with threats forcing them to give up their lands in Mississippi and move west of the Mississippi River.

Jackson explained to the chiefs that white Mississippians outnumbered Indians by five to one. Perhaps he exaggerated, but his next statement, that the majority of white Mississippians lived on only one-third of the land area while the Indians still controlled two-thirds of Mississippi, was unquestionably true. Only the southern third of the state, stretching from the Mississippi to the Alabama line, and a small half-moon-shaped section between the Tombigbee River and the Alabama line were then open to settlement.

In the land-hungry settler's view, that situation was grossly unfair. Settlers viewed the Indians largely as shiftless thieves who preferred stealing livestock to raising it. The Indians, of course, resented the increasing number of squatters who illegally moved onto their lands and refused to be evicted.

At first the Indian leaders at Doak's Stand proved reluctant, but Jackson's combination of threats and promises finally worked. He promised them thirteen million acres in Arkansas and Indian Territory in present Oklahoma for their five million acres in central and western Mississippi. He promised food, household goods, guns, and ammunition to those Indians who agreed to move west. With the Indians still loath to agree, Jackson shifted tactics. He lectured them angrily, warning that this was their last chance. If they rejected the offer, he implied, they faced only two alternatives—extinction or forcible removal. It worked. The chiefs, though still objecting, signed. By the terms of the Treaty of Doak's Stand, the Indians gave up a huge tract of fertile land spreading over west-central Mississippi.

Mississippians celebrated, but only momentarily, for in north and eastern Mississippi the Choctaws and Chickasaws still retained their homelands, encompassing roughly half the land area of the state. Furthermore, the Choctaws who lived in the Doak's Stand cession were not obliged to leave the state. They were only encouraged to do so. The events at Doak's Stand cracked the door to Indian removal, and those who favored the complete obliteration of Indian lands in Mississippi and the removal of all Indians to the west, found encouragement. Within fifteen years, they gained complete victory.

By the late 1820s, the pressure became too heavy for the Choctaws and Chickasaws to withstand. In 1829 Andrew Jackson, long a proponent of Indian removal, assumed the presidency of the United States. Thus was opened a new avenue of attack, and the Mississippi Legislature quickly pursued it. On January 17, 1830, the Mississippi lawmakers approved legislation removing the autonomous rights of the Indians who remained in Mississippi. By extending the protection of Mississippi laws and government over the Indians, the politicians, in reality, told the Indians that, to save their tribal government and to maintain their tribal freedoms, they must leave Mississippi and head west to Indian Territory. This new coercion succeeded. Before the year was out, meeting with U.S. government representatives at Dancing Rabbit Creek in eastern Mississippi, the Choctaws ceded the remainder of their lands and agreed to a tribal exodus to new lands in Indian Territory. Two years later, the Chickasaws, long noted for their stubbornness and independence, capitulated, and in the Treaty of Pontotoc Creek agreed to similar terms.

The Indian cessions tripled the public lands available for settlement and provoked explosive changes for the state of Mississippi—changes that pushed Mississippi onto a divergent course. Embryonic institutions and ideals most at odds with the dreams of many other Americans flourished. As the nation moved toward industrialization, Mississippi's agrarianism prospered. As the nation became more critical of slavery, Mississippi's slave population zoomed upward, thus making it increasingly difficult for Mississippians to criticize the institution. Other characteristics more in keeping with American ideals withered. Education, beginning to thrive in the rest of the nation, remained dormant in Mississippi. The promising development of some urban life was curbed by the availability of cheap new public lands. Towns like Natchez, Vicksburg, and Jackson failed to grow, a pattern that for a century after 1830 would keep Mississippi one of the most rural states in the nation. Mississippi was becoming peculiar—and therefore isolated from the rest of America.

The first change came in the 1820s in the immediate aftermath of the Doak's Stand cession. The sudden opening and sale of these fertile lands in west-central Mississippi and the lower Delta spurred a land rush that strengthened the power of the backwoodsmen and weakened the influence of Natchez and the old river counties. Within the ten years after 1820, nearly thirty thousand people flocked into the Doak's Stand cession. They represented about 22 percent of the state's total population. Developing a political coalition with their backwoods neighbors in the piney woods, they wrested political control from the river counties.

One of the first demands of the new backwoods coalition was to move the state capital, situated at Natchez, to a more central site. In 1821 the legislature commissioned Thomas Hinds, James Patton, and William Lattimore to seek out a site for a new seat of government. The legislators specified a number of criteria. First, the site had to be within thirty miles of the exact geographic center of the state. It had to be on a navigable stream and accessible by road. It must be situated on high, healthful ground. After a thorough search, the commissioners recommended LeFleur's Bluff on the Pearl River, the site of a Choctaw trading post. Although the site was not within thirty miles of the center of the state, it fit the other requirements, and the legislature approved. Frame structures were erected and the government moved to the new capital in December 1822. Not coincidentally, the legislators named the new capital Jackson, honoring their backwoods hero and the architect of the Treaty of Doak's Stand, Andrew Jackson. In the 1820s and 1830s, Andrew Jackson's popularity among Mississippians was unshakable.

The rush into the Doak's Stand cession, important as it was in strengthening the backwoods, proved to be only a prelude. In the 1830s, a political, economic, and social transformation occurred after the much larger cessions of Dancing Rabbit Creek in 1830 and Pontotoc Creek in 1832. Suddenly the northern half of Mississippi came open to settlers and speculators. The results were immediate and profound for the future of Mississippi.

New immigrants flocked to north Mississippi, some to expand the cotton frontier, others to speculate in the cheap and abundant public lands. In the ten years between 1830 and 1840, Mississippi's population increased 175 percent. Slave population increased 197 percent; and by 1840, for the first time, blacks outnumbered whites in the state. These were rates of growth unequalled in Mississippi history. Between 1833 and 1836, the legislature organized thirty new counties, all in the newly ceded Choctaw and Chickasaw lands. Public-land sales boomed. Five public-land offices between 1833 and 1837 sold seven million acres, much of it bought by speculators who used a minimum of hard money and an unlimited supply of credit to accumulate paper fortunes. The federal government set the price of $1.25 per acre for minimum blocks of eighty acres. In the single year of 1835, public-land offices in Mississippi disposed of nearly three million acres. The backwoodsmen, now thoroughly in command of the legislature, chartered bank after bank to furnish the credit to fuel the boom. The only asset possessed by many of the new banks was a printing press to crank out banknotes, which in turn were backed by the land that borrowers bought with the banknotes. This cycle seemed to produce unlimited prosperity for all. Land prices continued to climb. Towns sprang up overnight. Free-wheelers, lawyers, charlatans, gamblers, speculators descended into Mississippi to make fortunes. Mississippi in the 1830s was a preview of California in the 1849 gold rush or Tulsa in the oil boom of 1901.

Perhaps the best description came from a young Virginia lawyer who settled for a time in Alabama and Mississippi. Joseph Glover Baldwin gave the era of the 1830s its name—"Flush Times." Settlers, he explained, came from "all quarters of the Union, especially from the slave-holding states." They came with high hopes, little hard money, but a plentiful supply of optimism and brass. Armed with a law book and sent on his way by "the gentle momentum of a female slipper," Baldwin gave as explanation for his own migration from the Old Dominion the

> magnificent accounts . . . from that sunny land of most cheering and exhilarating prospects of fussing, quarrelling, murdering, violation of contracts, and the whole catalogue of *crimen falsi*—in fine, of a flush tide of litigation in all of its departments, civil and criminal . . . a legal Utopia, peopled by a race of eager litigants, only waiting for the lawyers to come on and divide out to them the shells of a bountiful system of squabbling.[1]

For the man on the make, Mississippi was a paradise. Speculation in the cheap lands was rampant. As Baldwin described it,

> Money, or what passed for money, was the only cheap thing to be had. . . . Credit was a thing of course. To refuse it . . . were an insult for which a bowie-knife were not a too summary or exemplary means of redress. The State banks were issuing their bills by the sheet, like patent steam printing press *its* issues; and no other showing was asked of the applicant for the loan than an authentication of his great distress for money.[2]

In such a society, he noted, "prices rose like smoke. Lots in obscure villages were held at city prices; lands bought at the

1. Joseph G. Baldwin, *The Flush Times of Alabama and Mississippi* (New York: D. Appleton and Company, 1853), p. 83, pp. 47–48.

2. Baldwin, *Flush Times,* p. 83.

MISSISSIPPI

A photographer's essay by Bruce Roberts

COHN BROS.
EST. 1875
OLD COUNTRY
DRY

Chevron
KIMMIE
TEMPORARY
ASSIGNMENT

LEE RD.
BEAUREGARD RD.
STOP

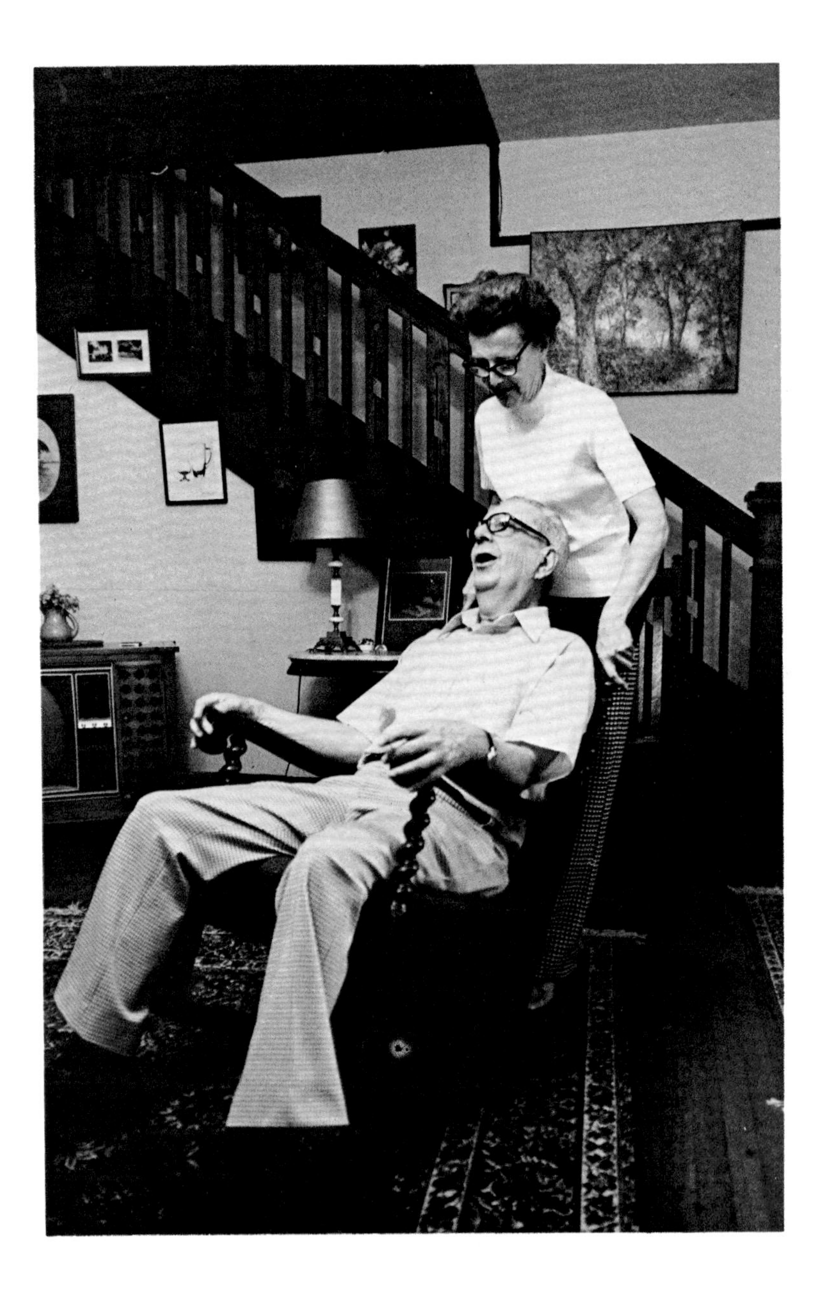

Photographs in sequence

Flowers and cannon, Vicksburg National Military Park.
Country store on Route 61, north of Natchez.
Antebellum mansion, Natchez.
Old courthouse, Vicksburg.
Man and cannon, Vicksburg National Military Park.
Oil refinery worker, Pascagoula.
Shipyard worker, Pascagoula.
Oil refinery, Pascagoula.
Boat harbor and beach, Biloxi.
Sand sculpture, Gulfport—Biloxi area.
Cotton field near Greenville.
Biloxi beach at low tide.
Walter and Elizabeth Perry, Hattiesburg.
Amusement park, Gulfport.
Mississippi River from bluffs near Natchez.

minimum cost of government, were sold at from thirty to forty dollars per acre, and considered cheap at that." [3] Nobody inquired into origins or qualifications. According to Baldwin,

> . . . some unscrupulous horse-doctor would set up his sign as "Physician and Surgeon," and draw his lancet on you, or fire at random a box of his pills into your bowels, with a vague chance of hitting some disease unknown to him, but with a better prospect of killing the patient, whom or whose administrator he charged some ten dollars a trial for his markmanship.[4]

Another observer, the Yankee traveler Joseph H. Ingraham, remarked on the great number of young men he encountered idling and conversing on the streets of small Mississippi villages. The traveler, he said,

> . . . will find every third building occupied by a lawyer or a doctor, around whose open doors will be congregated knots of young men, *en deshabile* [*sic*], smoking and conversing . . . sitting upon the counters or lounging about the doors. In the streets and barrooms of the hotels, they will cluster around him, fashionably dressed, with sword canes dangling from their fingers. . . . Whole classes from medical and law schools, or whole counting-houses from New-York or Boston, seem to have been transported *en masse* into the little village through which he is passing.[5]

But the boom could not last. In 1837, just before leaving the presidency, Andrew Jackson issued the Specie Circular, a treasury order to the land offices ordering them to accept nothing but hard money in payment for public lands. The land bubble burst. As land prices plummeted, wildcat banks and speculators went broke in droves. Sheriffs were "as busy as a militia adjutant on review day" [6] serving foreclosure notices. Often they could only scribble "G. T. T. (Gone to Texas)," across the backs of the notices, for many speculators and settlers simply left their debts behind, to start over again farther west.

3. Baldwin, *Flush Times*, pp. 83–84.

4. Baldwin, *Flush Times*, p. 89.

5. Joseph H. Ingraham, *The Southwest by a Yankee*, 2 vols. (New York: Harper and Brothers, 1835), 2:168.

6. Baldwin, *Flush Times*, p. 91.

Yet there was a more serious and permanent side to developments within Mississippi in the 1830s. Jacksonian Democracy triumphed, and the egalitarian tenets of that faith became a permanent fixture. The Constitution of 1817 inevitably came under attack as being far too conservative to suit the new backwoods order. By 1832 the democrats of the interior already had gathered enough strength to force a change, and in that year the legislature called elections to choose delegates for a new constitutional convention. The outcome of their efforts was the Constitution of 1832, a document that embodied the most perfect statement of frontier democracy ever adopted by a southern state. As the convention opened, one delegate wrote to a friend, "You may . . . rest assured that we will give you a constitution . . . much more *democratic* than any other in the U.S. Not *republican*—but downright and absolute *democracy*." [7]

His promise was not achieved without a struggle. The majority were vocally democratic new men from the backwoods. Most had little governmental experience. John Anthony Quitman, an Adams County delegate, lamented that "the many young and inexperienced men we have in this body gives rise to extravagant and wild schemes." A few days later he wrote his wife that "those who possess least ability to instruct are ever foremost in debate." [8]

That the frontier democrats would have their way despite the doubts of the delegates from the river counties was never in doubt. At the 1832 convention, the election of judges symbolized the fight between backwoods Democrats and river-county conservatives. Delegates from the river counties, derisively called "aristocrats," saw the Jacksonian belief in elective judgeships as rampant mob rule—a provision that would, if adopted, politicize the bench and promote partisan justice. The backwoods Jacksonians, called "whole hogs," favored the election of all public officials, even judges. A small group, the

7. Stephen Duncan to Levin Wailes, September 14, 1832, Wailes Papers, Mississippi Department of Archives and History, Jackson, Miss.

8. John Anthony Quitman to Mrs. Quitman, Quitman Family Papers, no. 616, Southern Historical Collection, University of North Carolina Library, Chapel Hill, N.C.

"half-hogs," favored the election of lower-court judges and the appointment of supreme-court judges.

The "whole hogs" won on all issues. The Constitution of 1832 proclaimed universal white manhood suffrage and ended property qualifications for holding office. Life tenure was ended; all offices now must be filled by election to specific terms. Governors, placed on a two-year term, could serve no more than four years out of any six. Interestingly, the Constitution of 1832 prohibited the introduction of slaves into Mississippi as merchandise after May 1, 1833, and allowed the legislature to forbid the introduction of slaves after 1845 even by their owners. These restrictive provisions were never enforced, and therein lies another story of change.

By 1830 slavery and the plantation system were firmly entrenched only in the river counties. True, slavery was developing also in the fertile counties of the Doak's Stand cession. By no means in 1830, however, was it inevitable that slavery would grow, prosper, and spread. Nor was it inevitable that Mississippians would embrace the institution, as they did before the decade ended, and make slavery the only acceptable answer to the questions brought by a large black population. In the 1830s, Mississippians changed their attitudes toward slavery. When the decade began, they viewed the institution as a necessary evil. By 1840, Mississippians defended it as a positive good.

The number of slaves grew dramatically during the 1830s. In that decade, Mississippi's slave population increased from 66,178 to 196,577. Only 20,940, or approximately 16 percent, of that statewide increase occurred in the seven oldest river counties where the plantation system was already established. Neither was the increase dramatic in the red-clay hills of north-central Mississippi nor in the counties of the northeast. A positive decline in both white and black population occurred in the piney-woods counties. Slavery burst out of its confines of the southwestern counties, following cotton culture into central Mississippi and the lower delta. Furthermore, slavery became immensely profitable in the fertile new cotton lands. The fact that Mississippians became stubborn defenders of slavery between 1830 and 1840 is not difficult to explain. First, Mississippians feared that white society would be overwhelmed, increasingly outnumbered as they were by black slaves. Second, and not surprisingly, they found intellectual, psychological, and moral justification for a system that proved so economically profitable. It is hardly remarkable that white supremacy swept Mississippi in the 1830s. Neither, perhaps, is it amazing that those thought patterns lasted so long, outliving the Civil War and Reconstruction and forming the ideological foundation for resistance to the civil-rights movement more than a hundred years later.

Mississippi politics, too, took on a new and colorful style, reflecting the growing class divisions between Whig river counties and Democratic backwoods. In 1839 Sargent S. Prentiss, Whig candidate for Congress, appeared on the stump to debate Democratic gubernatorial candidate A. G. McNutt. McNutt admitted Prentiss's brilliance, but deplored the Whig candidate's love of liquor. Prentiss mounted the stump in reply:

> My fellow-citizens, you have heard the charge against my morals, sagely, and, I had almost said, soberly made by the gentleman, the Democratic nominee for the chief executive office of this State: had I said this, it would have been what the lawyers term a misnomer. It would be impossible for him to do or say anything soberly, for he has been drunk ten years; not yesterday, or last week, in a frolic, or socially, with the good fellows, his friends, at the genial and generous board—but at home, and by himself and demijohn . . . selfish and apart from witty men, or ennobling spirits, in the secret seclusion of a dirty little back-room, and on corn-whiskey! . . .
>
> Now I will admit, fellow-citizens, that sometimes, when in the enjoyment of social communion with gentlemen, I am made merry with these, and the rich wines of glorious France. It is then I enjoy the romance of life. Imagination, stimulated with the juice of the grape gave to the world the Song of Solomon, and the Psalms of that old poet of the Lord—glorious old David. . . . Now, fellow-citizens, during this ardent campaign . . . I have only been drunk once. Over in Simpson County I was compelled to sleep in the same bed with this distinguished nominee . . . and in the morning I found myself drunk of corn-whiskey. I had lain too close to this soaked mass of Democracy, and was drunk from absorption.[9]

9. Sparks, *Memories*, pp. 355–356.

Prentiss's speech, facetious though it was, tells much about the divisions and style of antebellum Mississippi politics. It shows a personal quality, a politics of personality, that has characterized the state ever since. From Prentiss to Bilbo, it has never been enough for Mississippi politicians to have a program or ideals; they must display a personal color and style. Often, indeed, the color and style has camouflaged a lack of goals. Prentiss's diatribe also humorously reflects an aristocrat-small farmer dichotomy, roughly reflected in a pervasive east-west sectionalism that stretches from territorial days through the first half of the twentieth century.

In the 1830s and 1840s, that division was Whig versus Democrat, river-county planter-conservative versus interior yeoman-small planter radical. That traditional cleavage became more firm in the 1830s. In that decade, the split was manifest in such issues as the Constitution of 1832 and the promotion of easy-credit, easy-money economic policies. Two decades later, the same divisions are reflected in the drive toward secession: the Whigs of the western counties remained Unionists, while the Democrats became Secessionists. The Delta planter-hill farmer conflicts of the late nineteenth and early twentieth centuries is a more recent reflection of the same phenomenon. As in slavery and white supremacy, Mississippi's political divisions too were set in the 1830s for the next hundred years.

Frederick Law Olmstead, a New York traveler and journalist, journeyed through Mississippi in 1853 and 1854. As he rode through Wilkinson and Adams counties, he remarked on the wealth and sophistication of the local planters. His book, *A Journey in the Back Country,* was written for the readers of Olmstead's New York newspaper. Upon reading it, one gets the impression that the author's purpose was to explain a foreign land to his readers. The Mississippi he saw was mainly a land of vast cotton plantations worked by gangs of fifty to a hundred slaves and presided over by semiliterate overseers in the employ of rich barons who spent most of their time luxuriating in their Natchez mansions or in Europe.

Another traveler, John F. H. Claiborne, a nephew of former territorial Governor W. C. C. Claiborne, in 1841 completed a similar journey through the piney woods of southeastern Mississippi, and, like Olmstead, Claiborne reported his impressions to the readers of his newspaper, the *Natchez Free Trader and Gazette*. Claiborne found a different world from that described by Olmstead. Claiborne described a society as much different from that of the Natchez nabobs as the latter were different from the Pennsylvania Dutch farmers. Claiborne encountered few planters, little cotton, and rarely did he see slaves. In Wayne County, as Claiborne rode alone toward Natchez nearly two hundred miles away to the west, he found himself at nightfall lost in a thunderstorm. Luckily, he rode up to a frame house in the pine forest. It was the home of a widow and her family of four daughters and three sons. The sons were absent on a cattle drive. The widow took the drenched, exhausted Claiborne in for the night. Claiborne's description is instructive. He found the house unpretentious but neat, clean, warm, and comfortable. When he stabled his horse, his hostess filled the feeding trough with sweet potatoes and hay made of sweet potato vines, which the horse "ate . . . with great relish." When he sat down to supper,

> The repast was abundant, excellent and scrupulously neat—but almost every dish was composed of [sweet] *potatoes* dressed in many various ways. There were baked potatoes and fried potatoes—bacon and potatoes boiled together—a fine loin of beef was flanked round with potatoes nicely browned and swimming in gravy. A hash of wild turkey was garnished with potatoes. . . . A roast fowl was stuffed with potatoes, beside us stood a plate of potato biscuit, as light as sponge; the *coffee,* which was strong and well flavored, was made of *potatoes,* and one of the girls drew from the corner cupboard a rich potato pie. In about an hour, a charming blue-eyed girl brought us a tumbler of potato beer that sparkled like champagne.[10]

When he turned in for the night, "the bed itself, though soft and pleasant, was made of *potato vines*. . . . we rested badly; the night-mare brooded over us; we dreamed that we had *turned into a big potato* and that some one was *digging us up*." [11]

10. John F. H. Claiborne, "A Trip through the Piney Woods," *Publications of the Mississippi Historical Society* 9 (1906):533.

11. Claiborne, "The Piney Woods," pp. 533–534.

When he awoke with a sore throat, his host applied a plaster made of sweet potatoes and vinegar and served him tea brewed from potato vines. As the family sent him on his way, they filled his pockets with preserved sweet potatoes.

Claiborne's experience comes closer to the truth for most Mississippians than Olmstead's. Yet Olmstead's version persists that most Mississippians were planters who surveyed large acreage worked by gangs of slaves; that all efforts were directed toward the single cash crop of cotton; and that because of the obsession with that commodity, planters imported pork, corn, and other necessary supplies from the free states to feed themselves and their slaves. Only one other group invades that picture. The poor whites, according to the traditional story, formed a degraded, landless, lazy class, pushed off the better lands onto the infertile red-clay hills.

Contemporary travelers like Frederick Law Olmstead were fascinated by the planters and equally unimpressed by the small farmers. One traveler who wrote a widely circulated account of his travels in Mississippi used the following words to describe the yeomen: "sullen or insulting," "destitute of . . . morals, education, and reverence for religion," "rude and ignorant." [12] So did the literary romantics of post-Civil War days glorify the planter and demean the yeoman. Hollywood and tin-pan alley strengthened that belief through movies like *Birth of a Nation* and *Gone With The Wind* and the songs of Al Jolson.

Mississippians themselves embraced the myth of the lost cause. They wanted to believe that a grand and noble society had in fact been lost because of the Civil War. As Aristotle noted, in true tragedy one must fall from a high estate. Historians, too, perpetuated the myth. The great planters left records, diaries, journals, and account books. Farmers seldom did. Using only the written sources, historians, not themselves immune to the romanticism of the plantation myth, furnished an unbalanced account of society in antebellum Mississippi. Before the Civil War and into modern times, most Mississippians were farmers, not planters. Most people did not own any slaves, and

12. Ingraham, *Southwest,* pp. 171–172.

even among those who did, most owned fewer than ten. Hence, in the 1830s another pattern emerged that was to dominate the history of the state for the next hundred years—that of the yeoman farmer who worked his own land and depended as much on livestock and subsistence crops as he did on cotton.

Certainly great planters existed, especially in the western half of Mississippi. Yet even there, where plantations were most numerous, qualifications must be made. A study made in 1945 by Herbert Weaver [13] indicates that in the western counties, the richest soil region in the state, planters, those who owned more than two hundred acres and twenty slaves, numbered only 45 percent of agricultural operators. Even among those, most had risen to planter status in their own lifetimes. Most had come into the state in the 1830s and 1840s and by reinvesting their profits had managed to accumulate sizable land and slaveholdings by 1860. Nor did they partake of the pretensions of the planter class. Even the travelers who visited antebellum Mississippi remarked on the absence of mansions, except in Natchez. The typical planter lived in a frame dwelling with undeveloped grounds, surrounded by slave quarters and outbuildings made of logs. Planters and farmers lived side by side with few social, political, or economic divisions separating them. Except for the wealthiest Natchez planters, and they were perhaps more capitalists than agriculturalists, Mississippi planters held egalitarian social views.

In the northeastern third of the state, the planter class was hardly numerous enough to exert influence. There, in some of the most populous counties in the state, the planter class numbered no more than 15 percent of agricultural operators. Sixty-one percent were slaveless, yet most of these owned sizable farms.

In the southeast pine barrens, by 1860 the most sparsely populated area of the state, planters could hardly be found. Great planters comprised less than 1 percent of agricultural operators, and small planters numbered about 8 percent. About 63

13. Herbert Weaver, *Mississippi Farmers, 1851–1860* (Nashville: Vanderbilt University Press, 1945), pp. 40–42.

percent of the agricultural operators in the area were nonslaveholders, but only 22 percent owned no land. Again, just as in the northeast, many slaveless farmers owned their own farms.

For the state as a whole, perhaps 20 percent of Mississippi farm operators were planters. Not more than 8 percent ranked as great planters—those who owned 50 or more slaves and more than 500 acres of improved land. By far the dominant class numerically was the yeoman class—those independent small farmers who owned fewer than 200 acres of improved land and either a few slaves or none at all. Statewide, the yeoman almost certainly numbered 60 to 70 percent of Mississippi's white population. Among Mississippi farmers in 1860 slightly more than half owned no slaves. Another 20 percent owned fewer than ten; fewer than 6 percent owned more than 50. Mississippians in the generation before the Civil War were farmers, not planters.

The tremendous increase in Mississippi's population in the antebellum generation came almost entirely from immigration. In the thirty years before 1860, Mississippi's population increased from 136,621 to 791,305. Almost all of the new Mississippians came from the older states of the South. One historian estimated that of all the farmers in Mississippi in 1850, only 12 percent were born in Mississippi; 83 percent had been born in the states of the older South. Only 5 percent came from the North or were of foreign birth. North Carolina furnished the most Mississippians; South Carolina, Tennessee, Virginia, Georgia, Alabama, and Kentucky ranked in order behind North Carolina. No foreign influences served to diversify and liberalize the state. From the boom of the 1830s, Mississippi developed socially as a province of the older South, and perhaps, like most provinces, she felt a need to defend and conserve the values of the mother states.

The coming crisis of the new order began to accumulate in the 1840s. In that decade, national events combined to confront Mississippians with the necessity of defending slavery. In 1845 the annexation of Texas by the United States precipitated war with Mexico. At the end of that conflict, the nation acquired vast new territories including California and the Southwest. Immediately the question arose—should the new territories be slave or free? Thus Americans confronted the question, never satisfactorily answered, that twelve years later resulted in secession and civil war—should slavery be allowed to expand? Mississippians and their slave-state neighbors answered with a resounding and somewhat threatening yes. The superficial unanimity with which Mississippians defended slave expansion, however, masked some deep and fundamental internal differences that emerged in 1849 and lasted into the Civil War. With the rise of the abolition movement and the increasing popularity in the North of the Free-Soil position dedicated to the containment of slavery in those states where it already existed, Mississippians felt forced to choose a course to counter what they viewed as Northern provocation. From the first crisis in 1850 to secession in 1861, only two choices seemed to exist—union or disunion. How Mississippians divided in their choices is the story of the 1850s.

The sectional struggle began in 1846, even as the Mexican War progressed. In that year, President James K. Polk asked Congress to appropriate $2 million for peace negotiations with Mexico. Congressman David Wilmot of Pennsylvania attached an amendment to that appropriation requiring that slavery be forbidden in any territory acquired from Mexico. Although it never passed, the Wilmot Proviso stirred passions and promoted emotional outbursts from Southern slaveholders. When the war ended and the United States acquired California and the Southwest, the issue still smoldered. By 1850 the dispute burst into flames and produced a full-blown secession crisis. In that year, Congress faced the problems of admitting California as a free state and of organizing the remainder of the Mexican Cession into the Utah and New Mexico territories. The question once again surfaced—slave or free? Congress chose compromise. California would be admitted as a free state; the Utah and New Mexico territories would be organized without mention of slavery.

The controversy created a crisis in Mississippi. Mississippians had staunchly supported the Mexican War in the hope that slave territory would be expanded. Suddenly to confront the possibility of their peculiar property being excluded from the lands that they had helped win enraged them. Two heroes of that war attempted to mobilize Mississippi against the congressional compromise. John Anthony Quitman, Natchez planter, lawyer-politician, recent military governor of Mexico City, and in 1850 governor of Mississippi, was the most outspoken partisan of Southern expansionism. The other defender of state rights and vocal opponent of compromise in 1850 was sitting in the United States Senate. Jefferson Davis had proved his valor in Mexico as regimental commander of the famed Mississippi Rifles. Both men favored secession if the Free-Soilers successfully pressed their attempts to exlcude slavery from new territories.

Other Mississippians, however, were inclined to accept the congressional compromise. Senator Henry Stuart Foote, Davis's irascible senatorial colleague, stood for the Union. Foote and other Unionists hardly differed from the Secessionists on the questions affecting slavery; they simply believed that the institution could best be protected within the Union, safely shielded by constitutional guarantees.

In 1850 the dis-Unionists in Mississippi apparently held the upper hand. Quitman sat in the governor's chair and Secessionists controlled the legislature. Two elections would settle the issue in 1851. Under Quitman's urging, the state legislature issued a call for elections to a state convention to meet in the fall of 1851. Quitman hoped for a Secessionist majority that would carry Mississippi out of the Union. Also the biennial gubernatorial election came up in the same year. Quitman, the Secessionist, would oppose Foote, the Unionist. The Secession forces lost both contests. The first blow came in September 1851, when state voters selected delegates to the state convention. The Unionists won 57 percent of the vote and the majority of the delegates. Chagrined, Governor Quitman withdrew from the gubernatorial contest in disgust, and Jefferson Davis returned from his Washington Senate seat to replace him as the Democratic nominee. The contest could hardly have been a better referendum on secession, for Davis and Foote had been colleagues in the Senate a year earlier when the Compromise of 1850 was presented. Davis had opposed the compromise, and Foote had supported it. Foote won the governorship in 1851 over Davis by 999 votes out of almost 60,000 votes cast. The Unionists rejoiced, for the crisis seemed over.

In reality, the Unionist victory in Mississippi only represented a momentary interval in the agitation over slave expansion. Nationally, too, the issue had hardly been put permanently to rest by the congressional Compromise of 1850, as events in 1854 demonstrated. In that year, Congress organized the Kansas and Nebraska territories, and under the urging of Stephen Douglas attempted to dodge the slave issue by endorsing the doctrine of popular sovereignty. That solution allowed free immigration into the new territories by Free-Soilers and slaveholders alike, thus postponing any decision on slavery until statehood. At that time the Kansans and Nebraskans themselves would settle the issue.

Instead of calming the issue of slave expansion, the Kansas-Nebraska Act unsettled the question once more, this time in a more dangerous and virulent form than ever before. Kansas became the battleground. Slaveholders and Free-Soilers immigrated, some with the encouragement of their state legislatures, hoping to capture Kansas for their respective positions. Violence occurred between proslave and antislave settlers. Eventually, two state constitutions were proposed, one protecting slavery and one prohibiting it. Congress was again on the spot, and that body refused to accept either, thus postponing statehood until after 1861.

Other events of the 1850s aggravated the issue and strengthened the appeal of the forces of disunion. In 1857 the Dred Scott decision by the United States Supreme Court favored the position of proslave advocates. In that opinion, the justices declared flatly that slaves were property and that Americans could take their property anywhere they pleased. Thus, the Supreme Court implied that slavery could not be prohibited anywhere. Even in victory the proponents of slave expansion found hidden defeat, for the decision was simply ignored or defied by antislave forces, a reaction more galling to Southerners than if the decision had never been rendered in the first place.

In 1859 the abolitionist John Brown temporarily captured a federal arsenal at Harpers Ferry, Virginia, and called for a great slave uprising in the South. Nothing could have terrified and enraged slaveholders more.

Such great national events dominated the minds of Mississippians in the 1850s, and in every instance, from Kansas to John Brown, Mississippians' perceptions of these disputes strengthened the forces of disunion. Secessionists, discredited after their defeat in 1851, were creeping back to power by the mid-1850s. Jefferson Davis and Albert Gallatin Brown, both Secessionists, returned to seats in the United States Senate. John Anthony Quitman, along with Brown perhaps the most hotheaded of Mississippi fire-eaters, went to the House of Representatives. The last three governors before the war spoke forcefully for secession—John J. McRae, William McWillie, and John J. Pettus.

Mississippi newspapers filled their pages with emotional diatribes against abolition, bloody reports of the persecution of slaveholders in Kansas, and appeals to fear. Simultaneously, politicians hammered away at Mississippi slaveholders and nonslaveholders alike. Slavery, they emphasized, was essential, not only for economic reasons, but for social purposes, as well. They charged that the ultimate objective of both Free-Soilers and abolitionists was the destruction of slavery. These enemy forces already had control of the national Congress. Should they capture the presidency, all would be lost. Secession, they argued, was legal and, if necessary, could be accomplished without war. They pictured for their readers and listeners a North laid economically and socially prostrate by the denial of cotton supplies from the South and by the withdrawal of Southern markets for Northern goods.

Albert Gallatin Brown, former governor of Mississippi and United States senator at the time of secession, argued that the perpetuation of slavery not only was of paramount concern to the slaveowners but also was equally essential to nonslaveowners. Economically, he argued, nonslaveholders had as much monetary interest in slavery as those who owned slaves. Economic fortunes of both groups were so intertwined that prosperity for one meant affluence for the other. The reverse, he noted, was also true. The abolition of slavery would break the fortunes of the slaveholder and nonslaveholder alike. But he saved his most emotional appeal to the nonslaveholder for the social defense of slavery. Should slavery be abolished, slaveowners would flee the country and the nonslaveowning population would be left at the mercy of a large and uncivilized black population. Brown prophesied a grim future, should that occur.

> The negro will intrude into his presence—insist on being treated as an equal—that he shall go to the white man's table, and the white man to his—that he shall share the white man's bed, and the white man his—that his son shall marry the white man's daughter, and the white man's daughter his son. In short that they shall live on terms of perfect social equality. The non-slaveholder will, of course, reject the terms. Then will commence a war of races such as has marked the history of San Domingo. An unequal war, because it will be a war in which the negro and his Northern friends will stand on one side, and the non-slaveholder, deserted by the slaveholders, will stand on the other.[14]

While a great many Mississippians looked upon the rantings of the Secessionists as pure demagoguery, those who opposed secession differed hardly at all with their opponents on questions of white supremacy and the need for territorial expansion. They did differ on the best method of preserving and protecting the institution. They noted the Free-Soilers' promise not to molest slavery in those states where it already existed. They maintained further that slavery could be best protected within the Union by the shield of the constitution. By inviting war and destruction, Unionists argued, secession would almost certainly prove to be counterproductive and result in the ruin of the very institution the Secessionists were trying to save. Those who took that position were largely old Whigs from the plantation counties along the river. They had long distrusted the Democrats as demagogues, and secession to them was just another manifestation of Democrat hotheadedness. Furthermore, like most wealthy people, the great planters defended the *status quo*. They found strange allies in nonslaveholding farmers of small acreages from the counties of the northeast and the piney

14. Quoted in Percy L. Rainwater, *Mississippi: Storm Center of Secession, 1856–1861* (Baton Rouge: Otto Claitor, 1938), pp. 147–148.

woods. Mississippians hardly approached the fateful years of 1860–1861 with unanimity.

The national Whig party broke up over the slave issue in the mid-1850s. Out of the wreckage emerged the new Republican party, dedicated to the Free-Soil position and strong only in the North. When Abraham Lincoln, a Free-Soiler from Illinois, received the party's nomination for the presidency in 1860, the state Democratic convention of 1859 had already resolved

> that in the event of the election of a Black Republican to the Presidency, by the suffrages of one portion of the Union only, to rule over the whole United States, upon the avowed purposes of that organization, Mississippi will regard it as a declaration of hostility, and will hold herself in readiness, to co-operate with her sister States of the South, in whatever measures she may deem necessary for the maintenance of their rights as co-equal members of the Confederacy.[15]

The only hope for averting a confrontation was to maintain a united Democratic party and nominate and elect a candidate acceptable to both North and South. That was not to be, and, indeed, the most rabid Secessionists would have been disappointed had such occurred. By 1860 Mississippi's most radical Secessionists, like Albert Gallatin Brown, were Southern nationalists and slave expansionists, who dreamed of a great slave empire stretching over the American South, the Caribbean, Mexico, and Central America. They wanted an excuse to mobilize public opinion overwhelmingly in favor of separation. By refusing to accept Stephen Douglas of Illinois as the Democratic nominee and walking out of the convention, Mississippi Democrats helped to split the party at the very moment when it most needed unity. By mobilizing the states' votes in favor of John C. Breckenridge, the nominee of the Southern Democrats, they guaranteed the election of Lincoln. Mississippi Unionists attempted to mobilize support for John Bell of Tennessee, an old Whig who stood for compromise within the Union, but they were too late. Breckenridge carried the state with 40,797 votes. Bell ran second, with 25,040. Douglas, the Northern Democrat,

15. Rainwater, *Mississippi: Storm Center,* p. 99.

garnered only 3,283 votes. No Lincoln electors appeared on the Mississippi ballot.

With the election of Lincoln in November 1860, only the mechanics and tactics of secession had yet to be carried through. One tactical question remained—should Mississippi start secession machinery immediately, or should she await the actions of her sister states? Soon after Lincoln's election, Governor John J. Pettus met with Mississippi's congressional delegation to debate that question. Ironically, only Jefferson Davis, later to become the Confederacy's president, counseled delay. All others recommended an immediate call for elections to a state convention.

On December 20, 1860, the day South Carolina passed her Ordinance of Secession, Mississippians went to the polls to choose county delegates for a constitutional convention to consider the question of secession. The canvass for delegates to the convention proved less than perfect as a secession referendum. Many candidates left their positions on the question unclear during the campaign. Only one county convention instructed its delegates to vote for immediate secession. Many candidates called themselves simply co-operationists, a term that could cover any position from co-operation with the other slave states for secession to co-operation within the Union. Historians have labored long hours attempting to find patterns that would link the attitudes of the delegates to all sorts of different factors. Votes at the convention have been statistically correlated with wealth, slaveholding, geography, state of birth, and age. None of the data seems satisfying. No particular overriding pattern emerges.

Only a single generalization can be made. The wealthiest planters in Mississippi tended toward Unionism. Certainly not all great planters in Mississippi opposed secession. But most surely did. Their reasons are not hard to surmise. At the top of the economic and social ladder, Mississippi's largest planters had the most to lose from secession and war. Moreover, the great planters probably took a more realistic view of the relative strengths of the two sections than did their more isolated country cousins. Some of them had traveled in the North, had few illusions about the wealth and power of that section. Many, too, had an economic stake in the Union. Natchez nabobs like Stephen Duncan were not just great planters; they were capitalists who regularly invested their surplus capital in Northern banks and railroads. A disproportionate number of Mississippi's great planters had immigrated as young men from Northern or border states, where they still had family and friendship ties. The only other defense of the Union came from small farm counties where slaveholding was negligible—counties like Tishomingo in the northeast and Jones in the piney woods.

It is hardly astounding that the great planters and merchants from the towns and counties along the river stood for the Union. It is astonishing that the small slaveholders and nonslaveowners of the interior were made to believe that their destinies were linked to the preservation and expansion of slavery. Still, there were reasons. They feared the free Negro as an economic competitor. The yeoman farmer's interest in slavery certainly was more social than economic. He feared that emancipation would bring down white society. Given the choice between secession and abolition, such white Mississippians almost to a man preferred secession. The wealthy planter with at least the illusion of greater security believed there were other options. But those with small slaveholdings and many nonslaveholders by 1860 had come to see only two choices: annihilation of their way of life, or independence.

One hundred delegates gathered in the hall of the Mississippi House of Representatives in the capitol at Jackson. They convened on January 7, 1861, and from their first meeting, control rested in the hands of the immediate Secessionists. William S. Barry, Lowndes County Secessionist, defeated James L. Alcorn, Coahoma County planter and Unionist, for the presidency of the convention. On the first day, Barry appointed a committee of fifteen to draft an ordinance of secession. Named chairman of that committee was L. Q. C. Lamar, law professor at the University of Mississippi and immediate Secessionist. Lamar came to the convention thoroughly prepared, having already drafted an ordinance that he could draw from his coat pocket at the proper time.

The co-operationist forces, knowing they could not win in a straight fight with the Secessionists, decided to delay. On January 9, Lamar offered his ordinance dissolving the union between Mississippi and the United States. In a countermotion, J. Shall Yerger, Washington County Whig, offered a substitute "providing for the final settlement and adjustment of all difficulties . . . by securing further guarantees within the present Union."[16] Yerger's motion failed by a vote of twenty-one to seventy-eight. A second effort to trim the Secessionists came from James L. Alcorn. His proposal urged the postponement of Mississippi's secession until the states of Georgia, Florida, Alabama, and Louisiana had seceded. That proposal also failed; the vote was twenty-five to seventy-four. One final attempt at delay came from Walter Brooke of Warren County. On a question of such enormity, he argued, the people should be allowed to speak. He proposed a statewide referendum to be held on February 2, 1861. Brooke's motion, too, failed by a margin of twenty-nine to seventy. The final question came in the evening of January 9, 1861, and passed by a vote of eighty-four to fifteen. Even though all but two of the Unionists relented and signed the ordinance, their leaders still hoped to carry the issue to the people in the biennial state elections scheduled for the fall of 1861. Of course, the war made that plan impossible. Behind the rather predictable maneuvering at the convention lay more than a decade of rising emotion.

Historians have sought all sorts of rational motives for secession. Some have pointed to the doctrine of state rights—the South's belief that the constitution was a compact among states, not a contract among the American people. Others have pointed to the increasing economic divergence between an industrial and commercial North and the agricultural South. No doubt there is some merit in these arguments, and, certainly, they were voiced by many Mississippians. Yet in Mississippi these arguments, even when they were used, seemed to be rationalizations for the root issue—a rising emotionalism growing out of slavery. Mississippi Secessionists, however much they talked of state rights

16. Rainwater, *Mississippi: Storm Center*, p. 209.

or the protection of Southern agriculture, swept the state along on a tide of emotion. Rather pugnaciously, Mississippi's leaders by 1860 saw themselves as defenders of the honor, pride, and manhood of their state. Mississippians, belligerently independent, proud, and stubborn, were saying to the North, "Don't push us around. We'll fight." In a state where personal affronts were settled on the duelling grounds, Secessionists viewed the sectional conflict as an affair of honor—a duel raised to the sectional level. As Congressman Reuben Davis warned his Northern colleagues in the House,

> We will resist. . . . We will sacrifice our lives, burn our houses, and convert our sunny South . . . into a wilderness waste. . . . at the hazard of bringing upon the world bankruptcy and ruin, famine and pestilence, lamentation and mourning. . . . We will not be driven one inch beyond where we now stand; we will be butchered first. . . . Gentlemen of the Republican party, I warn you. Present your sectional candidate for 1860; elect him as the representative of your system of labor . . . and we of the South will tear this Constitution in pieces, and look to our guns for justice . . . against aggression and wrong.[17]

Before the Secession Convention adjourned, the members adopted "A Declaration of the Immediate Causes Which Induce and Justify the Secession of the State of Mississippi from the Federal Union." The opening paragraph sets forth the following introduction: "Our position is thoroughly identified with the institution of slavery—the greatest material interest of the world." Then, like the American Declaration of Independence, the authors set forth the abuses and provocations suffered by the slave states at the hands of the abolitionists. Secessionists tended to categorize anyone with doubts about slavery as an abolitionist, failing to see the vast chasm that separated the Free-Soilers from the abolitionists—failing to distinguish between an Abraham Lincoln and a William Lloyd Garrison. The entire Declaration of Causes deals with slavery. Not one word of it talks about state rights or economic differences. Mississippi Secessionists obviously saw themselves as new American revolutionary pa-

17. Rainwater, *Mississippi: Storm Center*, p. 94.

triots. The peroration, too, was designed to link their cause with that of the founding fathers. "Utter subjugation awaits us in the Union," the delegates argued. "We must either submit to degradation . . . or we must secede from the Union," they continued. "For far less cause than this our fathers separated from the crown of England." [18]

So by the end of the antebellum years, Mississippi's altered institutions, so rooted in the 1830s, had brought her to Armageddon. White supremacy embodied in slavery had become by 1861 the only tolerable answer for a white population outnumbered by blacks. Ironically, however, as black Mississippians came increasingly under more formal and restrictive oppression, white democracy and egalitarianism flourished. By 1861 Mississippi was a land of yeomen, who ironically marched away to a war for slavery—a war that was opposed by the largest slaveholders. Parts of the Mississippi mind were set in the generation before the Civil War—the tendency to react emotionally when the racial *status quo* was threatened, the touchy pride and the glorying in persecution, the intransigence in the face of provocation. Another part—poverty and defeat—would be set by the onrushing war.

18. *An Address Setting Forth the Declaration of the Immediate Causes Which Induce and Justify the Secession of Mississippi from the Federal Union and the Ordinance of Secession* (Jackson: Mississippian Book and Job Printing Office, 1861), pp. 2–5.

5

An Interregnum

THE Civil War came to Mississippi early, for the state occupied a strategic spot in Union planning. Located in the heart of the lower South, with the Mississippi River twisting along her western border, Mississippi provided for the Union the key to unlock Confederate control of the river and thereby divide the lower South. Coupled with that important strategic consideration was the emotional fact that Mississippi was among the most hotheaded of Secessionist states. If the Union leaders needed any further motivation for their troops, they could remind them that Mississippi was the home of Jefferson Davis, President of the Confederacy.

The battle for Mississippi opened in 1862 alongside the Tennessee River at Shiloh Church, north of Corinth, and ended with the surrender of General Richard Taylor's forces in early May 1865. The war came to Mississippi in three waves—the battles for Corinth-Iuka in the summer of 1862, the Vicksburg campaign from the fall of 1862 to July 4, 1863, and the battle for north Mississippi in 1864.

In February 1862 the first Confederate line of defense crumbled as Union forces under Commodore A. H. Foote and General Ulysses S. Grant took Fort Henry on the Tennessee River and Fort Donelson on the Cumberland. General Grant then moved up the Tennessee River and disembarked his army at Pittsburg Landing, opposite Shiloh Church. The war lapped at the northern border of Mississippi, for despite Grant's location twenty miles north of the Mississippi border, his aims lay in the extreme northeastern hills of Mississippi—specifically the Confederate Army of forty thousand, located at Corinth under Albert Sidney Johnston and P. G. T. Beauregard, and the Memphis and Charleston Railroad. That thin rail line formed an important east-west link to the Confederacy—a communications and logistical link almost as valuable as the Mississippi River. From Memphis, the line ran across extreme northeast Mississippi from Corinth to Iuka and thereafter followed the south bank of the Tennessee River across north Alabama to Chattanooga. There the railroad branched. One fork went south to Atlanta and branched again there to Charleston and Savannah. Another branch linked Chattanooga to Richmond. These stakes led the two armies to Shiloh, the greatest battle of the war up to that time. Tactically a draw (the Confederates won the first day, and the Union won the second), Shiloh was a strategic victory for the North, with the Union army remaining in place as the fighting ended. At the end of the two-day battle, the Confederates had failed to dislodge Grant from his position at Shiloh Church, thus opening northeast Mississippi to Union invasion. Corinth was evacuated by the Confederates on May 30, 1862.

From there the focus shifted to Vicksburg. By the summer of 1862, the Union gunboats ran unhindered in the Mississippi River except for the batteries dominating the four miles of water under the Vicksburg bluffs. Through the fall of 1862 and spring of 1863, Grant puzzled over ways to get his army into the relatively open country behind Vicksburg. At times the problem must have seemed as insurmountable as the precipitous bluffs that sheltered Vicksburg along the Mississippi and Yazoo rivers. Flanking actions to the north proved unsuccessful because of the flooded Delta country. That Grant wrestled with his problem for nearly a year before taking the fortress shows both his tenacity and the almost impregnable position of the Confederate defenses. After attempting several unsuccessful schemes to bypass the river defenses, in the last days of April 1863, Grant simply ran his gunboats and transports past the river batteries and ferried his army across the Mississippi south of Vicksburg.

By May 19 he had driven the Confederates from Jackson, defeated them at Champion Hill, and invested Vicksburg. Six weeks later, the besieged city fell. With it went the western half of Mississippi. The east remained unconquered. Through 1864 General Nathan Bedford Forrest thwarted all Union attempts to clear east Mississippi. Even when the war ended, that section was not fully secured by Union forces.

That Mississippians did not support the war with unanimity was indicated by the opposition to secession in 1861. As the war progressed, and especially after Union armies invaded the state, white dissent grew. Added to the opposition of the great planters were increasing numbers of Union sympathizers and Confederate deserters in the northeastern hills and piney woods. Both areas had relatively small slave populations, and the inhabitants objected vociferously to the 1862 Confederate conscription law that exempted persons reponsible for twenty or more slaves.

The Civil War cost one-half of all Mississippians mightily. For a moment it freed the other half from bondage. Slaves fled from their owners as Union armies approached. Some 17,000 Mississippi blacks joined the Union forces. Some even fought at Vicksburg. Yet the Union failed during the war to develop a consistent policy of dealing with the freedmen, leaving that attempt to postwar reconstruction. The war devastated Mississippi's economic, social, and governmental institutions. Thousands of young men trooped gaily away to war in fiercely named units like the Tippah Tigers, the Benita Sharpshooters, the Chunky Heroes, the Yankee Terrors, the Buena Vista Hornets, and the especially fearsome Oktibbeha Ploughboys and Tullahoma Hardshells. Many died. Approximately 78,000 men from Mississippi served in the Confederate forces. Thirty-six percent did not live to return. Approximately 12,000 fell in battle and 15,000 died of disease. The war riddled whole units. The Vicksburg Cadets marched off with 123 men; 6 came back. The Vicksburg Sharpshooters left with 124 and 1 returned. In single battles, the slaughter was enormous. The Sixth Mississippi Regiment went into the Battle of Shiloh with 425 men; 300 became casualties. At Antietam, the Sixteenth Mississippi regiment lost 63 percent of those present, and the Twenty-Ninth Mississippi lost 53 percent of those who fought at Chickamauga.

Of the men who lived to come home, many returned on one leg or minus an arm. Travelers remarked in 1865 and 1866 on the great number of amputees they encountered in travels through the South. In 1865 the legislature ordered a survey to be made "to ascertain the number of maimed State and Confederate soldiers in each county in this State requiring artificial legs." The same act ordered a study of "the practicability of establishing a manufactory" of artificial limbs "at some convenient point in this State." [1]

The next year the lawmakers appropriated $30,000 to pay for artificial limbs. Only $20,000 was appropriated for the state university. In 1865, 20 percent of all state revenues was earmarked for the care of destitute and disabled veterans and their families.

Wartime destruction of physical facilities—buildings, railroads, towns, and villages—was capricious. In a state that was 95 percent rural and agrarian, the contending armies could hardly destroy the principal asset, land. Certainly railroads in the Civil War held great strategic and logistical importance, and heavy and systematic destruction occurred along the main rail routes. Towns like Jackson, burned so completely by Union forces that it became known as "Chimneyville," suffered greatly. Vicksburg, bombarded for months by Union artillery and gunboats, needed considerable repair at war's end. The few factories that dotted Mississippi's landscape were among the prime objectives marked for destruction by Union forces. Even rural folk unfortunate enough to reside in areas of military campaigning had their food stores and means of livelihood "requisitioned." Confederates and Federals alike coveted draft animals and horses for use in supply trains or as cavalry mounts.

But the greatest destruction was institutional, not physical. In all respects—governmentally, economically, educationally, and socially—Mississippi was leveled. Slavery as a system of labor and a system of social control over the black population was

1. *Laws of Mississippi*, 1865, pp. 156–157.

demolished. Planters now without capital, labor, or work animals retrogressed to the status of yeomen. The University of Mississippi, opened in 1848 and just rising to regional prominence before the war, closed, its faculty to return to the North and its students to go to war. A similar fate doomed public education at the local level. Governor Charles Clark's arrest and the closing of the wartime legislature by Union forces in June 1865 left Mississippi without civil government. In short, out of the destruction of war, Mississippians faced an opportunity to develop a new order to replace the old, to recognize that their old institutions had led them to divergence and disaster, and to start anew. Or they could reaffirm the old order, perpetuate and defend in the face of defeat as many of the antebellum institutions as possible.

Hardly had the fighting ended before Mississippi's white leaders gave their answer, and after the interregnum of Radical Reconstruction, the answer became even more defiant: Mississippi would reaffirm and re-embrace the old institutions under different names. Sharecropping and the Jim Crow system provided the same economic and social controls over the freedmen that slavery had furnished before the war. Mississippi's dependence on cotton was perhaps greater after the Civil War than before. The state became neither more industrialized nor more urban, neither more cosmopolitan nor less suspicious and insular. Now, after the war, added to her reaffirmation of the antebellum order was another condition, frustrating and embittering: a grinding poverty for whites and blacks alike. The Civil War and Reconstruction changed permanently none of Mississippi's antebellum institutions.

The process of reaffirmation began in the last six months of 1865. Before Union soldiers expelled him from office, Governor Charles Clark asked two respected prewar Mississippi Whigs, both loyal Unionists, to journey to Washington, there to meet with President Andrew Johnson and determine the requirements for Mississippi's readmission to the Union. When William L. Sharkey and William Yerger arrived, the president refused to receive them as official emissaries from Mississippi, but he did agree to meet with them informally and privately.

Johnson's terms were simple, straightforward, and quick. First, he said, he would appoint Sharkey provisional governor. Next, those Mississippians who were qualified voters before secession and who would take an oath of allegiance to the Union could choose delegates for a constitutional convention. That convention, the president urged, should renounce slavery. Later, in August 1865, as the state convention met, President Johnson telegraphed two more suggestions. The convention should grant the vote to a limited number of freedmen, perhaps, he suggested, based on some literacy or property qualifications. Finally, he recommended, the convention should ratify the Thirteenth Amendment to the United States Constitution, thereby proving the state's good faith in abolishing slavery. Johnson hoped by quickly reconstructing the former Confederate states under his own terms to undermine the rising power of the congressional Radicals who favored a harsh and punitive Reconstruction. If Mississippi and the other seceded states could fulfill Johnson's terms before the end of 1865, the president could present the 1866 Congress with a *fait accompli.*

The plan went awry in Mississippi. Mississippi's Reconstruction convention, which convened in August 1865, was the first to be held by a former Confederate state. Hence, Mississippi's actions would be crucial to the future of Johnson's Reconstruction plans and significant in his increasingly rancorous relations with radicals who ever more stridently challenged the whole idea of presidential Reconstruction. The convention, despite its domination by pre-war Whigs, dodged President Johnson's recommendations. The delegates reaffirmed the Constitution of 1832, only adding a proviso prohibiting involuntary servitude and recognizing that slavery had been "destroyed" in the state of Mississippi. The convention also declared the Ordinance of Secession "null and of no binding force." On the crucial question of civil rights for the newly freed slaves, the convention took no position, declaring that question properly to be the prerogative of the legislature. Perhaps most important for the future, the delegates refused even to consider Johnson's suggestion of some sort of limited voting rights for freedmen.

If President Johnson was only mildly displeased with the

Mississippi convention's actions, he soon would see his whole blueprint for Southern Reconstruction destroyed by the activities of Mississippi's first postwar legislature. That body's miscalculations would not only lead Mississippians to re-embrace slavery under a different name, but would undercut entirely Johnson's position with Congress. Certainly, the slaves had been freed, but no authority had yet set the status of the freedmen. The Mississippi legislators assumed, erroneously, that they, not the federal government, would legally define the economic, social, and political rights of their former slaves.

The first postwar legislature met in early November 1865 at Jackson, in the full belief that Reconstruction was over. In part because of that body's actions, it was only beginning. In rapid succession through November and December Mississippi's lawmakers took actions that convinced many in the North that the Radicals were right: Mississippians had learned nothing from the war. They were, it seemed to many Northerners, casting defiance in the face of defeat, attempting to re-establish the old antebellum political, economic, and social orders under new names.

A few days before the lawmakers convened, newly elected Governor Benjamin G. Humphreys, a former Confederate general, spoke both to the defeated citizens of Mississippi and to the victorious North. His speech was double-edged. White Mississippians, he told the North, accepted the verdict of the war. He left little doubt, however, that white Mississippians expected to set the rules by which the freedmen would live.

Governor Humphreys began by reaffirming the belief in state rights—that the federal government exercised only those powers not reserved to the states or to the people. But, he continued, he had never believed that secession was constitutional, and even those who did must now recognize that the question had been decided by "the arbitrament of war. . . . a tribunal from which there is no appeal."[2] Despite rumors to the contrary, he argued, Mississippians accepted the destruction of slavery in good faith, and they were ready now to pursue economic recov-

2. *Journal of the Senate of Mississippi*, 1865, p. 16.

ery. On the question of the freedmen he spoke firmly and unequivocally.

> Several hundred thousand of the negro race, unfitted for political equality with the white race, have been turned loose upon society; and in the guardianship she may assume over this race, she must deal justly with them, and protect them in all their rights of person and property. The highest degree of elevation in the scale of civilization to which they are capable, morally and intellectually, must be secured to them by their education and religious training; but they cannot be admitted to political or social equality with the white race. It is due to ourselves—to the white emigrant invited to our shores—and it should never be forgotten—to maintain the fact that ours is and shall ever be a government of white men. The purity and progress of both races require that caste must be maintained.[3]

For the good of the freedmen and for the economic rehabilitation of the state, the former slaves must be required to work. So that the planter could be assured of reliable, long-term labor, Humphreys suggested yearly contracts between freedmen and planters.

Thus the Mississippi legislators, encouraged by Governor Humphreys and convinced of their legal right to do so, set about defining the role of the freedmen. Already most white Mississippians assumed that to grant any political rights to the freedman was pure folly. The legislature dealt with the problems of the freedman—his legal rights, his economic status, and his social rights. In three sweeping acts, all passed in the last days of November 1865, the state of Mississippi laid down the basic laws to govern the freedmen. In an act ironically entitled "An Act to Confer Civil Rights on the Freedmen, and for other purposes,"[4] the lawmakers set out the freedman's legal rights and economic status. He could own property, but only in incorporated towns. He could sue or be sued in state courts, but only serve as a witness in cases where a freedman was one of the parties to the case, not in cases involving only whites. The heart of the legislation set the freedman's economic status. Every

3. *Journal of the Senate of Mississippi*, 1865, p. 17.
4. *Laws of Mississippi*, 1865, p. 82.

freedman was required to have a contract to labor by the second Monday of January 1866 and annually thereafter. Those without such a contract could be arrested as vagrants and their services sold to the highest bidder. Those freedmen who broke their contracts or ran away from their employment would be arrested and brought back.

Perhaps the most controversial legislation dealt with freedmen apprentices. Orphans of freedmen or freedmen under the age of eighteen could be apprenticed out to "some competent and suitable person . . . provided, that the former owner . . . shall have the preference."[5]

"An Act to punish certain offences therein named, and for other purposes" forbade weapons to the freedman. Neither could he engage in "riots, routes, affrays, trespasses, malicious mischief, cruel treatment to animals, seditious speeches, insulting gestures, language or acts, or assaults." Nor could he exercise "the function of a minister of the Gospel, without a license from some regularly organized church." He could not drink "spiritous or intoxicating liquors" except "that any master, mistress or employer of any freedman, free negro or mulatto may give . . . spiritous or intoxicating liquors, but not in sufficient quantities to produce intoxication." Section four read,

> Be it further enacted, That all the penal and criminal laws now in force in this State, defining offences and presenting the mode of punishment for crimes and misdemeanors committed by slaves, free negroes or mulattoes, be and the same are hereby re-enacted, and declared to be in full force and effect, against freedmen, free negroes and mulattoes, except so far as the mode and manner of trial and punishment have been changed or altered by law.[6]

Quite obviously, the legislators intended to re-enact the slave code.

This unfortunate legislation created a storm of criticism. Mississippi was the first state to form a postwar civil government under the Lincoln-Johnson plan of Reconstruction, and her passage of the "Black Code" confirmed what the Radicals had

5. *Laws of Mississippi*, 1865, p. 87.
6. *Laws of Mississippi*, 1865, pp. 165–166.

been saying all along—that the South was unrepentant, that Southerners could not be trusted to deal fairly with the freedmen, and finally that the South, left to her own devices, would return to slavery under a different name. Most immediately, Mississippi's actions, copied by other former Confederate states, cut the ground from under President Andrew Johnson. He had staked his entire plan of presidential Reconstruction on the moderation of states like Mississippi. Mississippi's passage of the Black Code sealed the doom of the lenient, nonpunitive Reconstruction policies of Lincoln and Johnson. Momentum now shifted to Congress—a Congress dominated by Radicals who desired a social, political, and economic revolution in the South. The nine years from 1866 to 1875 seemed to bring enormous change in Mississippi, but in the end they brought little more than bitter partisan fighting and momentary and illusory political power for the freedmen.

In 1866, increasingly under the whip of Radicals like Thaddeus Stevens and Charles Sumner, Congress refused to seat Mississippi's newly elected delegation, dooming Mississippi's first native postwar government. In 1867 Congress passed legislation that placed the former Confederate states under military rule. Mississippi, along with Arkansas, made up the Fourth Military District. The military governor's first duty was to register voters and arrange for elections to a constitutional convention. The federal government gave full political rights to the freedmen, thereby creating a black majority of almost six to five in Mississippi's electorate. The newly enfranchised blacks, led by Northern men who had come South, and many old prewar Mississippi Whigs, who hated the Democrats more than they feared the freedmen, began Republican rule. In 1868 the Republicans constructed a new constitution; in 1869 they won the elections to fill the offices created under it; and in 1870 Mississippi's first Republican administration took office.

The leaders of Mississippi's Republican party during Reconstruction belied the historical stereotypes that later emerged. According to the myth, carpetbaggers were venal, vulturelike opportunists who sought personal wealth at the expense of the native whites. Scalawags were traitors who allied with the blacks to gain a political power that they otherwise could not have achieved. The freedmen, according to common belief, were ignorant, illiterate pawns whose voting strength kept the other two groups in power.

But James L. Alcorn, Mississippi's first Republican governor, was a wealthy Delta planter who had been active in Whig politics before the war. Though he had opposed secession as a delegate to the 1861 convention, he fought for the Confederacy until 1863, when he retired to sit out the rest of the war on his Coahoma County plantation. Alcorn joined the Republicans, he said, because it more nearly suited his conservative economic and social views than did the Democratic party. Also, he argued, if moderates failed to join the Republican party, it would be dominated by radicals.

Adelbert Ames, Mississippi's best-known carpetbagger, could perhaps be accused of political naiveté, but hardly was he evil or corrupt. A New Englander and a Union general, Ames had served as Mississippi's last military governor before resigning in 1870 to take a United States Senate seat offered by the new Republican-controlled Mississippi legislature. In 1873 he was elected Mississippi's second Republican governor. Ames proved to be an honest politician with a missionary zeal to uplift the freedmen. But he failed to gauge the deep bitterness of Democrats toward former Union generals—especially those who had been elected to political office by black votes.

Blanche K. Bruce and Hiram Revels, both blacks, became United States senators during Reconstruction. John R. Lynch became a congressman. Hardly were they the ignorant buffoons pictured in the myth. Their literacy, ability, and honesty were attested even by Democrats. Revels, the first Negro ever to sit in the United States Senate, had been born of free parents in North Carolina in 1827. He came to Mississippi during the war to organize churches and schools for freedmen. A dignified and refined but retiring man, he was drawn unwillingly into politics. His real love was education, and after his short term in the Senate ended in 1871, Revels became the first president of Alcorn University, the state college for Negroes established by the Republicans. Bruce, who served in the Senate from 1874 to

1880, was the son of a Virginia planter and a slave mother. Nominally a slave but reared and educated as a planter's son, Bruce migrated to Mississippi in 1868 and embarked immediately upon a career in politics. In his Senate years, Bruce proved astute, honest, and popular with his colleagues. He was admired and respected by no less a Democratic stalwart than his senatorial colleague from Mississippi, L. Q. C. Lamar. After his term ended in 1880, Bruce held various patronage jobs in Washington until his death in 1898.

Perhaps the ablest of all Mississippi blacks in the Reconstruction years was John R. Lynch. The son of a white planter and slave mother, Lynch was reared at Natchez. He entered politics after the war and went to the legislature in 1870 at the age of twenty-two. Two years later he was chosen speaker of the house but immediately thereafter was elected to Congress. He served there for six years before retiring from active politics. Afterwards, he studied and practiced law and served in the army from 1898 to 1911, rising to the rank of major. From 1911 until his death in 1939 at the age of ninety-three, Lynch lived in Chicago, dividing his time between his law practice, Republican politics, and the writing of books on Reconstruction.

The Republicans from 1870 to 1876 generally pursued moderate policies. Taxes increased by 1400 percent, but that rise took place against an unbelievably low prewar base. Furthermore, at their peak Mississippi's taxes were never as great as those in certain agricultural states of the North. State expenditures increased, but Mississippi now financed a statewide public school system, a financial obligation the state did not have before Reconstruction.

The Constitution of 1868 mandated public schools for all children in the state, thus insuring the first statewide system of public education in Mississippi's history. Behind that constitutional provision lay two highly emotional issues—education for the freedman and the question of separate schools for the races. But by 1868 even most Democrats had reluctantly accepted the necessity for some rudimentary education for the former slaves, and their fire centered on the latter question of segregated schools. Although an effort was made at the Constitutional Convention of 1868 to mandate separate schools, that proposal was voted down. Neither the constitution of 1868 nor the legislative act of 1870, which established the system and financed it, made any mention of the question of segregation. Thus many whites assumed that the Republicans would force the children of both races into one system. They were wrong. Though the Republicans made no law on the question, separate schools for the races developed. The fact became even plainer when the Republicans established Alcorn University as the black counterpart to the University of Mississippi and appropriated equal sums of money for each.

From the beginning of Republican rule in 1870, the Democratic party fought to restore its prewar dominance. So long as Republican control in Mississippi had support in Washington, the Democrats had little hope of recovering power. In 1871 local Democrats in Meridian drove local Republicans from power, only to see federal troops restore the Republicans. A similar affair took place at Vicksburg in 1874; but by 1875 it was obvious that the Republicans in Washington would not indefinitely shield Mississippi Republicans from the wrath of the Democrats.

On that premise, Mississippi Democrats, led by James Z. George, chairman of the State Democratic Committee, and L. Q. C. Lamar, congressman from Mississippi's northeastern district, made plans in 1875 to drive the Republicans from office. Mississippians would vote in that year to fill all two-year offices, principally congressional seats and legislative posts. Adelbert Ames's Republican administration had taken office in 1874; thus the terms of the state's executive officers would not expire until 1878. If, however, the Democrats could capture the legislature, they could force the removal of Ames and his Republican colleagues by impeachment.

The George-Lamar plan was simple. First, by promising to protect the freedmen's civil rights, the Democrats would attempt to draw the black vote away from the Republicans. Next, those freedmen and scalawags who persisted in working for the Republican party would be intimidated. The plan of 1875 outwardly was only a partisan fight by the Democrats to unseat the

Republicans. More fundamentally, it represented an effort by the whites to place the freedmen once more under the political and social control of their former masters.

The Democrats determined to carry the 1875 elections by peaceful means, if possible, but by force and violence if necessary. In the summer of 1875, the campaign blazed almost to the point of racial-political war. Democrats organized and armed extralegal militia units. Against white Republican leaders, Democrats employed threats, intimidation, and sometimes violence, hoping to frighten their opponents into aligning with the Democrats or at the least into ceasing their political activity. Against black Republicans, the most effective instrument was economic reprisal. Outright violence erupted at Yazoo City, Clinton, Columbus, and a number of other sites. In these "riots," the death lists invariably included many more blacks than whites, more Republicans than Democrats.

Governor Ames, alarmed at the violence, attempted to organize black militia units to insure a fair election. Democrats saw that effort as dangerously provocative. Should black militia be used, they threatened, a race war would break out. Ames pleaded for federal troops, but President Grant, facing divisions in his own party over Southern Reconstruction, refused. He advised Ames, in effect, to handle the situation at home. Grant's refusal to intervene with federal force sealed the fate of the Republicans. In October Ames met with George and other leading Democrats, and they reached a one-sided agreement: Ames would cease organizing a black militia; the Democrats in turn would allow a peaceful election.

Election day came on November 3, 1875. The election proved neither totally fair nor completely peaceful. In Aberdeen, Democrats guarded the polls with a cannon. In Amite County, Democrats drove black voters from the polls. At Columbus, mysterous fires broke out the night before election day, and the frightened freedmen took to the woods. At Port Gibson, firing broke out at the polls. One Negro was killed, and four or five others were wounded. At Meridian, Negroes were allowed to vote only when accompanied by white Democrats. At most polling places, however, such tactics proved unnecessary, for economic pressure, threats, and pre-election violence had done their work. The Democrats swept the elections, winning majorities in both houses of the legislature and capturing five of the seven congressional posts. The turnabout in some hitherto heavily black Republican counties was amazing. In Yazoo County, Republicans cast only seven ballots and in Kemper County, only four. Both counties had been Republican strongholds in the elections of 1873. Democrats swept local offices in sixty-two of the seventy-four counties.

When the legislature met in 1876, the white Democrat majority proceeded to deal with the Ames administration. Ames's lieutenant governor, black A. K. Davis, was impeached and removed. Ames and T. W. Cordoza, the state superintendent of education, resigned under threat of impeachment. "Redemption," as the white Democrats called their *coup d'etat,* was complete. The Negro once more lay at the mercy of the white minority.

The legacies of Reconstruction in Mississippi furnished myths for the people to explain their poverty, shibboleths for Democratic politicians to use to stay in office, and a convenient explanation for worsening race relations. Reconstruction did not produce fundamental change. At its end, the black majority once more was headed for bondage, this time through sharecropping and Jim Crowism. Mississippi remained unindustrialized and rural, and cotton increased its hold on the state's economy. As one historian notes, "It has been almost as unfortunate for our nation that the North has remembered so little of Reconstruction as that the South has remembered so much." [7]

7. Hodding Carter, *The Angry Scar: The Story of Reconstruction* (Garden City, New York: Doubleday and Company, Inc., 1959), p. 12.

6

Farther Down a Different Road

IF Mississippians after Reconstruction returned to a variation on the antebellum racial theme, no less did they revive the mystique and sovereignty of cotton agriculture. Before the Civil War, cotton was Mississippi's chief cash crop. Agricultural and political leaders, nonetheless, often repeated the need for diversification; and despite their reliance on cotton as a cash commodity, prewar Mississippi farmers and planters raised great quantities of corn, sweet potatoes, cowpeas, and livestock. From the end of the Civil War through the Second World War, cotton tightened its grip on Mississippi's economy, both quantitatively and geographically. By 1890 cotton production had returned to the 1860 level of approximately 1.2 million bales. By 1929 Mississippians grew nearly 2 million bales. Counties that had grown little cotton in antebellum days, by the early twentieth century, were trying to produce it. Even in the piney woods and the northeastern hills, areas of poor soil where prewar farmers had never attempted to grow much cotton, farmers in the 1920s were trying to scratch cotton fields out of the sterile hillsides. In pre-Civil War days, Mississippi farmers grew as much corn as cotton and were largely self-sufficient in meat and vegetable production. In the eighty years from 1865 to 1945, those items declined steadily. Hence King Cotton not only was restored after the Civil War, he strengthened his sovereignty.

The labor system that evolved to replace slavery, was partly to blame for the increased dependence on cotton after the Civil War. Sharecropping proved hardly a material improvement over slavery for Mississippi blacks. In the immediate aftermath of freedom, rumors circulated that the freedmen would receive lands and thereby gain economic independence from their former white masters. Although many believed the rumors, the prospect remained only a dream; and even before the end of Reconstruction, Mississippi blacks once again had become economically subservient. They could not long retain their newly won political and social rights in the absence of economic independence. By 1890 slightly more than 10 percent of Negro farmers owned their own homes. Most blacks found themselves tied to the land as sharecroppers. They soon found that they had traded slavery for serfdom.

Sharecroppers were as much at the mercy of white landlords as slaves had been to their masters. Under the sharecropping system, blacks traded their labor for a subsistence. Families were assigned a usually ramshackle cabin in the middle of a cotton field. From the outset, they were beholden to the landlord for a "furnish," credit extended until the crop was harvested. The landlord told the croppers when and what to plant, when to hoe and pick, and, most important of all, he kept the books and sold the cotton against which the furnish was tallied. Almost always, the cropper found himself ever deeper in debt to the landlord. If the system was not exactly slavery, it certainly promoted economic bondage.

In the 1880s, pressures began to accumulate that would push Mississippi blacks even further into neo-slavery. The Democrats who had driven the Republicans from power in 1875 were more akin to prewar Whigs than to Democrats. Interested in plantation agriculture, finance, railroad building, and conservative economic policies, they rapidly made enemies of many small hill farmers. These conservative Democrats—led by lawyer-politicians like L. Q. C. Lamar, James Z. George, and Edward Carey Walthall—did not suddenly curtail the Negro's political rights. They merely controlled them. Democratic leaders shied away from overt efforts to remove the black man from politics, for such actions could bring down the wrath of the federal government in a renewal of Reconstruction. Then, too, the conservatives needed the blacks, for two reasons: first, they could use Negro votes to offset any defections from the Democratic faith by the hill farmers who increasingly criticized the conservative alliance with bankers, railroads, and Delta planters—the forces that the hill farmers recognized as their persecutors; second, the hill farmers could be held in line behind conservative policies by fears of renewed Negro domination. The black man once again, as in prewar days, was cast in the role of the fearful alternative to white unity. In election after election, the word went out: if the white man divides, the black man will take over. By 1890 that fear led to the beginning of the final political and social subjugation of Mississippi Negroes.

The Constitutional Convention of 1890 was called for a variety of reasons. Some believed the Constitution of 1868 to be tainted with Radical Republicanism. It was an instrument written by aliens and should therefore be junked. Others, like the hill farmers of the eastern counties, wished through reapportionment to unseat the conservative Democrats who had dominated the party since 1875. Still others wanted to curb the interests—the railroads, banks, and insurance companies. But centrally, the convention met to remove the black man from politics in Mississippi. By 1890 most white Mississippians not only believed that that should be done, but that it could be done without bringing about the intervention of the federal government. White supremacy, after all, by then had become entrenched in the North as well as the South. It was also increasingly clear that the North, frenetically engaged in industrial expansion, had little energy to spare to oversee the fate of a black peasantry in Mississippi. After all, few Negroes in 1890 lived in the North. Small hill farmers saw the political emasculation of Mississippi's blacks as absolutely essential. Only when the black man was reduced to political impotence could the hill farmers disrupt the Democratic party and unseat the conservatives. Conservatives themselves feared that they could not always control the black vote. As long as the Negroes voted, they would have to be controlled; and control meant fraud, intimidation, threats, and vote-buying. Only when the black man was no longer a political factor, the reasoning went, could the white man afford to conduct honest elections. As one member of the convention put it,

> Sir, it is no secret that there has not been a full vote and a fair count in Mississippi since 1875, that we have been preserving the ascendency of the white people by revolutionary methods. In other words we have been stuffing ballot boxes, committing perjury, and here and there in the state carrying the elections by fraud and violence. . . . No man can be in favor of perpetuating the election methods which have prevailed in Mississippi since 1875 who is not a moral idiot.[1]

The election for convention delegates took place in the summer of 1890. Outside the river counties, where black voters generally co-operated with white Democrats, only one black Republican offered himself for election. A few days after he began his campaign in Jasper County, his body was found peppered with bullets. Of the 134 delegates who assembled at Jackson in mid-August 1890, 130 were Democrats. The other four listed themselves as "Republican," "National Republican," "Conservative," and "Greenbacker." The Republican was the only Negro at the convention, Isaiah T. Montgomery—businessman, planter, and founder of the all-Negro community of Mound Bayou.

The main purpose of the convention, rewriting the franchise to exclude blacks, produced the most spirited debate. No differences arose over the necessity of disfranchising blacks. Even Montgomery acquiesced in the inevitable. Differences did arise over how it should be done. Conservatives wanted property qualifications that would be applied to whites and blacks alike. Small hill farmers, of course, objected to that scheme. Another alternative was a literacy test, but such a test applied equitably would exclude illiterate whites, as well as blacks. Piled atop that dilemma was the problem of possible federal reaction. In 1890, for the first time since 1875, the Republicans held both Congress and the presidency. Any restrictive provisions obvi-

1. *Jackson Clarion-Ledger*, September 11, 1890.

ously aimed at black voters would violate the Fifteenth Amendment to the Constitution, which guaranteed political rights to blacks. The convention faced a delicate problem.

The delegates solved the problem by writing an article on the franchise that seemed to apply to blacks and whites alike. Nowhere did the article obviously exclude black voters. One must look into the speeches of the delegates, the journal of the convention, and the newspapers of the day to find the real motive: to exclude blacks from politics while leaving loopholes through which white registrants could pass. The key provision was a literacy test. Carefully worded so as to allow illiterate whites to register but to exclude Negroes at the discretion of the county circuit clerks, the provision required that any prospective voter "be able to read any section of the constitution of this state; or he shall be able to understand the same when read to him, or give a reasonable interpretation thereof." [2] In addition to the literacy test, a prospective Mississippi voter under the Constitution of 1890 had to meet some of the lengthiest residency requirements and most complicated registration procedures in the country. If he had lived in the state two years and in his precinct for one year, he still was required to pay a two-dollar poll tax. Not only must he pay it, but he must pay it by February 1 in each of the two years preceding the election. Furthermore, he must keep his poll tax receipts and present them at the polls as proof of payment.

The new franchise provisions of the constitution of 1890 severely curtailed democracy in Mississippi. A new registration was required under the new articles before 1892, and Mississippians soon realized that if the new requirements cut Negro voting to almost nothing, they also kept many whites from the polls. In 1880, 110,113 whites were registered in Mississippi, and 130,607 blacks were on the rolls. In 1896, after reregistration under the new constitutional requirements, the number of black registrations shrank to 16,234. White registrations dropped only to 108,998. But if the white registrant slipped through the literacy test, the poll tax operated as heavily against

2. *Constitution of Mississippi,* 1890, Sec. 244.

him as it did against the blacks. In 1895, in a hotly contested, statewide election, only 64,339 voters went to the polls. Some were black, so it is apparent that only about half the white registrants voted. Obviously, many whites who were otherwise qualified to vote had failed to pay their poll taxes.

Inevitably, the new provisions went to court for review. In two cases, the Mississippi Supreme Court upheld the constitutionality of the franchise article. In both opinions, the court reasoned that, while discrimination might be possible under the new provisions, they were not designed to be discriminating. "It may be," the court admitted, "that their operation will be to exclude from the exercise of the elective franchise a greater proportionate number of colored than of white persons." Yet, the judges concluded, "this is not because one is white and the other is colored, but because of superior advantages and circumstances possessed by the one race over the other." [3] In 1898 the United States Supreme Court spoke. The Court agreed with the Mississippi Supreme Court in upholding the constitutionality of the franchise article. The Court stated, "They [the provisions] do not on their face discriminate between the races and it has not been shown that their actual administration was evil, only that evil was possible under them." [4]

Now freed from restraint by the national government, white Mississippians set about reducing their black wards socially and economically. Although some hints of Jim Crowism developed even during Reconstruction, segregation through law and custom was largely a development that occurred after the successful assault on the Negro's political rights in 1890. A law was passed in Mississippi as early as 1865 relegating freedmen to the second-class rail coaches; yet, when there, they sat side by side with white second-class passengers. The question of separate schools for the races was ignored by law, even by the Republicans during Reconstruction. Perhaps legal Jim Crowism as a cause for the black man's oppression has been exaggerated and extralegal segregation underestimated. Mississippi, as late

3. *Dixon* v. *State* 74 Miss. 271.
4. *Williams* v. *Mississippi* 170 U.S. 213.

as 1940, had only a few Jim Crow laws in the state code. No one, however, could argue that black Mississippians did not suffer oppression. It was, however, an oppression more enforced by custom than by law—custom that forced the black man in every respect to defer to the white man, to give way on the sidewalks, never to neglect the "sir" and "mister" in his addresses with whites, and—most important of all—never to show unusual ambition. For a black to aspire to wealth or position was among the most threatening actions he could pursue. Not only did the system deny economic opportunity, it positively pushed the Negro backwards. Blacks who emerged from slavery skilled in the trades were driven into the ranks of the unskilled. Oftentimes they were elbowed aside by white competitors, even for the most menial jobs. One black from the piney woods tells of helping a white farmer put in a crop. His wages amounted to five dollars per month. After a month, he lost that job to a white man who agreed to work only for room and board. So the black man's position in Mississippi retrogressed in the last years of the nineteenth and the first three decades of the twentieth century.

By the turn of the century, however, black Mississippians held no monopoly on poverty and discrimination. Small farmers from the eastern hills—"Rednecks," as the planters soon called them—increasingly railed against a political and economic system that ignored their interests. A credit system that required the farmer to pledge his crop to the merchant to receive credit to produce the crop ground down the small farmer into the ranks of the sharecroppers. Sharecropping developed after the Civil War as a system of black labor. By 1930 half of Mississippi's sharecroppers were white. By 1900 a conservative political machine dominated state politics, favored the planter over the small farmer, and curried favor with the railroads, banks, and merchants by enacting favorable legislation and tax policies—in the mind of the small farmer, all policies favorable to his enemies. Before the twentieth century, the small farmers were helpless. Movements such as Populism, aimed at breaking the strength of the powerful special interests and making government more responsive to the common man, captured some plains states, but never came close to success in Mississippi. As long as the black man represented even a possible threat in Mississippi, white conservatives and radical small farmers were forced into an alliance of race—a coalition that defied economic self-interest. Among Mississippi whites, the race issue often has overridden economic differences. When the United States Supreme Court upheld the constitutionality of the suffrage provisions in the Mississippi Constitution of 1890, blacks were no longer a real political factor (although still, for white politicians, the Negro would have his psychological uses). White Mississippians tended to be most conservative and resistant to reform when the racial *status quo* was under attack, but by 1900 that issue seemed dormant. For the first time since 1830, the state faced the possibility of real change—change rooted in the grievances of small farmers who now determined to challenge the conservatives for control of the Democratic party.

In the first twenty years of this century, progressive reform had a chance in Mississippi. The movement was led by two of the most influential political figures in modern Mississippi history—James Kimble Vardaman and Theodore Gilmore Bilbo. Both were, in today's political terms, "liberals." They championed the economically and socially downtrodden. They advocated better public education, improvements in public health and penal reform, curbs on the power of big business, child-labor laws, better state care for the insane and the handicapped, and a host of other reforms; but at the same time, they were Mississippi's most notable racists. They advocated a progressivism for whites only. By attempting to uplift the poor whites without altering the status of Mississippi blacks, by then 60 percent of the population, they assured the failure of their programs. No more than white Mississippians of a later generation did the followers of Vardaman and Bilbo recognize the unbreakable link between black oppression and white poverty. They failed to realize that, as long as three-fifths of Mississippi's people remained economic, political, and social ciphers, all Mississippians would suffer.

In many ways James K. Vardaman—who rose to the governorship in 1904, then to the U.S. Senate in 1912, riding on the issue of small-farmer discontent—was the most amazing and contradictory figure in modern Mississippi politics. With little formal education, Vardaman read widely enough to win admission to the bar at age twenty-one. He was, however, to practice law only sporadically. Because he was related to the influential Money family of Carroll County (cousin Hernando de Soto Money became a United States senator), Vardaman settled at Carrollton, on the edge of the Delta. Fifteen miles away, at Winona, he began his law practice, but he soon abandoned the legal profession to edit the *Winona Advance.* From Winona he moved to Greenwood, a growing cotton-market town thirty miles west of Winona. There he bought the *Greenwood Enterprise,* soon making it the leading newspaper in the area. For more than a decade before he was elected governor in 1903, Vardaman's editorials chronicled his political, social, racial, religious, and economic beliefs. His opinions proved unorthodox and enlightened in many areas, and primitive in others. Although, early in his newspaper career, Vardaman's beliefs differed little from the positions of the conservative Democratic leaders of Mississippi, by the turn of the twentieth century he had become a progressive. The reasons for Vardaman's ideological transformation are uncertain. How much his new views were caused by deep conviction and how much came from political convenience is hard to judge. Yet it is certain that Vardaman's progressivism suited an increasingly vocal and politically powerful small-farmer faction in the Democratic party. So did his rabid racism. Whatever his motives, Vardaman's views were reformist and often contradictory. He abhorred capital punishment and yet justified lynching. At a time when Mississippi convicts were leased out to planters who worked them under the most brutal conditions, Vardaman called consistently for penal reform and rehabilitation of criminals. In a state where Baptist and Methodist ministers molded opinion even more than politicians, Vardaman challenged all blue laws and criticized the religious bigotry sometimes displayed by intolerant preachers. Tom Paine was one of his heroes. Politically, he favored almost all ideals of Progressives of that time—better education, public health, control of big business, primary nominations, freedom for the Philippines. Vardaman, in all respects, was at least as progressive as Robert LaFollette of Wisconsin and Hiram Johnson of California; and he was more radical than Governor Woodrow Wilson of New Jersey. Yet there was one monumental difference: Vardaman was the most notorious racist in Mississippi history, excepting only his successor, Theodore Bilbo. No doubt Vardaman's racism was a mixture of demagoguery and personal belief. His beliefs extended only to the black man, for he lambasted anti-Semites and praised the accomplishments of Jews. That he believed in white supremacy was not unusual, for most white Americans in his day did. That he felt it necessary to state his beliefs vociferously and emotionally at a time when Mississippi blacks were so impotent amazed even his contemporaries. He viewed the black man as subhuman and believed that to educate Negroes beyond the menial level only frustrated them and gave them dreams and expectations that they could never realize. Educating a black, he argued, "only spoils a good field hand." [5] Vardaman was not inconsistent, then, in his view that money used for black education should be given to whites.

Vardaman's views were anomalous enough that he could engage in such mental and moral gymnastics as editorializing against capital punishment, advocating lynching as the only proper punishment for rape of a white woman by a Negro male, and traveling two hundred miles shortly after becoming governor to save a Negro from a lynch mob.

Vardaman served as governor from 1904 to 1908 and as United States senator from 1912 to 1918. Called the "White Chief" by his hill-farmer followers, Vardaman, in four years as governor, produced more reform than was brought about in any other Mississippi gubernatorial term of modern times. Although the legislature balked at transferring money for Negro education to whites, Vardaman did manage to increase school appropriations by 20 percent and teachers' pay by 30 percent. He got a state textbook commission established to break the monopoly of

5. William F. Holmes, *The White Chief: James Kimble Vardaman* (Baton Rouge: Louisiana State University Press, 1970), p. 78.

the American Textbook Company. He pushed through regulatory legislation aimed at insurance companies, railroads, utilities, and banks. Since 1892, in Mississippi, manufacturing and banking corporations had been limited to real estate holdings of no more than $1 million in value. When the 1906 legislature voted to raise that limitation to $10 million, Vardaman promptly vetoed the legislation, noting that it would benefit only the great lumber companies and land speculators. Large landholdings, he argued, should be broken up, not allowed to increase. He advocated, but failed to get, a reduction of the legal interest rate, a state tuberculosis sanatorium for the free treatment of tuberculosis victims, a state school for the mentally retarded, and child-labor legislation.

But Vardaman's crowning achievement was reform of the convict-lease system. Since the end of Reconstruction, the state had leased convicts, mostly blacks, to private individuals. Usually, the convicts labored on private plantations or railroad construction. For the use of convict labor, the lease holders paid into the state treasury $1.10 per month for each convict. The leasee in return commanded the prisoners' labor and carried the responsibility of feeding, clothing, and housing the convicts. The system could hardly have been better designed to promote abuse, brutality, and neglect. Mortality among Mississippi convicts exceeded 10 percent annually. Between 1875 and 1904 the convict-lease situation became a long-standing but tolerated scandal. Not only did the system almost guarantee maltreatment of convicts, but the leasing arrangements were shot through with corruption and political favoritism. The Constitution of 1890 outlawed the practice of leasing convicts—a practice that nevertheless continued into Vardaman's term, under a slightly altered form. Vardaman, who believed that convicts should be rehabilitated rather than punished, determined to end the convict lease. Abolition of the system was the bitterest fight of Vardaman's governorship. The leasees, the politically powerful McLaurin brothers, fought the governor through the courts and through the legislature. Vardaman finally prevailed, when the legislature in 1906 agreed thenceforth to work the convicts only on prison farms, public roads, levees, or other lands owned by the state. The largest of these prison farms came to be Parchman, an 18,000-acre plantation in Sunflower County.

Even while he served as governor, Vardaman yearned to go to the United States Senate. Vardaman's cousin, Senator Hernando de Soto Money, chose not to run for re-election in 1907. Vardaman and John Sharp Williams of Yazoo County, a veteran of the U.S. House of Representatives, opposed each other for the seat. In one of the closest contests in Mississippi history, Williams eked out a victory. Vardaman's next opportunity came in 1910. His bitterest political enemy, Senator Anselm J. McLaurin, died in office in 1909. In 1910 a Democratic caucus of legislators, after six weeks of balloting amid charges of bribery and fraud, awarded the unexpired term to conservative Delta planter Leroy Percy. Vardaman and his followers were enraged, claiming that the will of the people had been thwarted by professional politicians. Vardaman wasted no time launching his campaign for the next full term. He easily defeated Percy and a number of other candidates. In 1912 he went to the United States Senate.

Vardaman served only one term. While in Washington, he aligned himself with the most progressive leaders. The crisis of Vardaman's senatorial career came with World War I. Convinced that the war was none of America's business and that it would halt progressive reform, Vardaman, along with only five other senators, voted in April 1917 against the American declaration of war. Although he knew he could not stop the stampede to war, the price Vardaman paid for his principle was his political career. Defeated for re-election by Pat Harrison in 1918, after a campaign that played heavily on Vardaman's antiwar views, the White Chief never again held political office. He died in 1930 at the home of his daughter in Birmingham, Alabama.

Vardaman's tragedy and Mississippi's loss was that, in the end, his racism not only obscured his reform accomplishments, it positively cancelled them. He sustained a peculiar mental compartmentalization that allowed him to ignore black poverty, black social problems, and the lack of black opportunity. Vardaman, like many later Mississippians, could neatly exclude blacks from his reform system, for blacks hardly counted—poverty was their natural state. Sadly, Vardaman never realized the inextricable economic and social bond between white Mississippians and blacks. So, in the end, despite reform rhetoric and some real accomplishments, progressivism in Mississippi failed to change anything fundamental. Like so much else in Mississippi history, the Progressive movement foundered on the race question.

The inheritor of Vardamanism was Theodore G. Bilbo. In belief, constituency, and progressive ideals, and in his use of racism, Bilbo was Vardaman's natural successor. Like Vardaman, Bilbo drew his strength from the small farmers of the eastern hills. Like Vardaman, Bilbo was a progressive reformer, placing in his platforms many of the social programs Vardaman had wanted and failed to get. Like Vardaman, Bilbo in his late career increasingly allowed his racial views to obscure his accomplishments. If there were similarities, there were also differences. For a principle, Vardaman sacrificed his career. Even his bitterest enemies had a sneaking admiration for Vardaman's idealism. Nobody questioned Vardaman's honesty. The same is not true of Bilbo. It is difficult, if not impossible, in Bilbo's case, to separate buffoonery from reality and personal ideals from opportunism. Bilbo began his political career amid charges of personal corruption and died in 1947, beseiged by charges of bribe-taking. Between those years, he served successively as state senator, lieutenant governor (1912–1916), twice governor (1916–1920, 1929–1932), and United States senator (1934–1947). Only his first gubernatorial term produced solid accomplishments. After that, his platform became Bilbo's election, and his notoriety served as his program.

As governor from 1916 to 1920, Bilbo brought Mississippi's progressive years to a close. Among his accomplishments were the creation of a state tax commission to equalize taxes, greater appropriations for public education, and the creation of a tuberculosis sanatorium. The country's entrance into World War I ended reform in Mississippi, as it did nationally. When Bilbo left the governor's mansion (which, as a symbol of aristocracy, both Vardaman and Bilbo advocated selling), so did Progressivism.

Certainly agrarian leaders had contributed much to change Mississippi. Vardaman and Bilbo personified aggressive action and political energy. Surveying the first twenty years of the twentieth century in Mississippi, one is struck by the political excitement of that era. In a state that traditionally appreciated political color and spice, the Vardaman-Bilbo years provided great political entertainment. But those years produced accomplishment, too. The first real social services provided by Mississippi began in the first two decades of the twentieth century. Public education, all but dormant since Reconstruction, got a financial boost, and most of Mississippi's institutions for the handicapped—the blind, deaf, retarded—date from the Progressive years.

Yet, by 1920, what had *really* changed? Economically, black Mississippians were still slaves. Politically, they wielded no power. Nearly nine Mississippians still lived in rural areas for every one who lived in a town or city. Farm tenancy and King Cotton dominated Mississippi agriculture more in 1920 than in 1870. Now not only was the black kept in economic bondage by sharecropping, but the white man was, also. Manufacturing employment increased somewhat in the period between 1890 and 1920, but almost all of the increase occurred in the sawmills of the piney woods. Manufacturing employment in 1920 still accounted for less than 10 percent of the labor force. The 1920s found Mississippians, in spite of the efforts of the agrarians and Progressives, still rural, still at the mercy of declining cotton prices, still wedded to tenancy, and still unable to solve the moral and economic dilemma posed by the race question.

In the 1920s, Mississippi was a forgotten state in a forgotten region. Nationally, the 1920s are usually described as the "roaring twenties." Mississippi hardly roared. Americans in the 1920s were more prosperous than ever before in the nation's history. Mississippians were poor. At a time when material comfort through the mass production of consumer goods became almost a national religion, Mississippians found themselves left out. With a per-capita income of $396, only one-third the national average, Mississippians little understood the moral arguments in the 1920s over America's worship of material things. The United States in the 1920s had already become an urban nation. The glamorous, growing cities were the magnets of the nation, attracting the bright and ambitious. America's cities in the 1920s became the country's newest frontier. Mississippi, meanwhile, remained overwhelmingly rural. In 1920, 86.6 percent of the state's citizens lived in the country. The 1920s for the United States were years of tremendous industrial growth and consolidation. Mississippi remained almost wholly agricultural. Six of every ten Mississippians lived on farms. Of those, 65 percent did not own their land; 68 percent of all Mississippi farms in 1925 were tenant-operated, and 60 percent of those tenants were sharecroppers.

Nor did the great social questions of the decade seem to affect Mississippi. Restriction of immigration could hardly be of much interest in a state whose population was almost wholly native-born. The debates over Darwin and evolution could hardly make a stir in a state almost completely Baptist and Methodist. Mississippians could not be expected to get very excited about the debate over prohibition. Mississippi, after all, was the first state to ratify the Eighteenth Amendment and the last to repeal it. Mississippi in the 1920s found herself left out, ignored by the nation, hardly mentioned in the national press, except for an occasional snicker at the state's backwardness or the notation of a lynching.

The Great Depression and Franklin D. Roosevelt's New Deal should have wrought a revolution in Mississippi, for out of hard times generally comes a willingness to experiment and to alter old patterns. The Great Depression harshly underlined the defects in Mississippi's economic order. Traditional reliance on agriculture as the chief employer and money-maker to the exclusion of even a modest industrial base made Mississippians particularly vulnerable to price changes in agricultural commodities. The disproportionate role that cotton played, as the sole crop in the agricultural sector, put Mississippians at the mercy of that commodity. Mississippi's economy hardly flourished in the 1920s, but cotton prices remained high enough through that decade for farmers to stay solvent. Cotton prices fluctuated in the twenties from twelve cents a pound to twenty-eight cents, usually hovering around twenty cents. In 1930 the price dropped to nine cents and in 1931 to five cents. Any farmer who owed money faced disaster. Financial institutions foreclosed mortgages by the thousands. Other farmers lost their land for failure to pay taxes. In the single year of 1932, mortgages were foreclosed on one of every ten farms in Mississippi. On a single day in April 1932, one-fourth of the land area of Mississippi was auctioned for unpaid taxes. Owners had two years to redeem their land by paying back taxes, so all were not immediately evicted. Nevertheless, those astounding statistics attest to the disaster of the depression in Mississippi.

Out of the calamity came the first realization by Mississippians since before the Civil War that the old institutions would no longer serve. Simultaneously, drives began for agricultural diversification and for industrial development. Neither was a new subject for Mississippians. Long before the Civil War, some Mississippians had lamented the tyranny of cotton when the prices went down and then had relied ever more heavily on it when the price went up. So too, there were attempts to develop industry, but in a state chronically short of capital, grassroots industrial growth seemed, at best, ephemeral; at worst, hopeless. In his inaugural address in 1874, Carpetbagger Governor Adelbert Ames criticized Mississippi's utter reliance on cotton. Mississippi, he said, was an economic colony. In true imperialistic fashion, she exported cotton and timber to the North and imported shirts, furniture, and other necessities. None of Mississippi's million citizens, he noted, was engaged in manufacturing. Sixty-five years later, in 1939, industrialist Governor Hugh L. White made a speech to the Kansas Chamber of Commerce. His remarks echoed Ames's. White, too, called Mississippi a colony. Mississippi ranked among the top three states in lumber production, White noted, but imported furniture and paper from the North. At that time, Mississippi claimed the largest tomato-shipping point in the nation, yet bought canned tomatoes and catsup from the eastern corporations. The greatest producer of cotton in the United States imported shirts from Massachusetts.

Although White was not the first to recognize the problem, he was the first seriously to attack it. In 1935, during his successful campaign for the governorship, White emphasized Mississippi's need to "Balance Agriculture With Industry," and in 1936 he shepherded his program through the legislature. BAWI, as the program was named, proved an innovative idea. Recognizing the impossibility of generating home-grown industry, White's premise was that industry should be attracted from outside. To draw industry into Mississippi, two things would be necessary—a public relations effort directed by the state and direct financial benefits. Industries agreeing to migrate to Mississippi under the plan could expect tax relief for a period of years. In addition, local authorities could issue bonds to build and equip plants that, in turn, industries leased from the municipality. Although the BAWI plan would have great impact on the state after World War II, it was launched in the midst of the greatest industrial depression in American history. While White's BAWI changed the state's economy little, before World War II, it did hold the promise of change.

The impact of FDR's New Deal on the state of Mississippi is uncertain. Surely Mississippians received attention from Washington that the citizens of the state were unused to. One suspects that the social reformers, particularly those in the Department of Agriculture, saw Mississippi as part of a great laboratory. They made efforts to uplift sharecroppers through the Resettlement Administration and Farm Security Administration. These efforts usually aimed at pulling the tenants upward toward being "forty-acres-and-a-mule" farmers. These efforts failed miserably. The federal government was attempting to perpetuate the small farmer at a time when mechanization and efficiency dictated ever larger agricultural units. Tenancy passed rapidly from the Mississippi scene in the next decade, but not because of the New Deal.

Mississippians also received more money from the federal treasury than ever before. Federal agricultural payments to planters hastened the end of tenancy, for instead of passing those benefits on to their sharecroppers, landlords often used the money to mechanize their operations. Cotton acreage was reduced; but because of greater efficiency, production declined hardly at all. Cotton in 1930 comprised 79 percent of Mississippi's cash receipts for field crops. It still accounted for 75 percent in 1939.

No historian has fully assessed the impact of the New Deal in Mississippi. When the era is thoroughly studied, we may find that the 1930s represent the first real break with the dominant themes and institutions that ruled Mississippi for the previous century—one-crop agriculture, poverty, insularity, and race. But one suspects not. The 1930s may have produced among Mississippians the realization that a transformation in the state's institutions was necessary, but there is little evidence that the decade produced much immediate change. In 1939 King Cotton still sat squarely on his throne. The ratio of blacks to whites stood in 1940 almost exactly where it had a hundred years earlier, and the complexities of race weighed as heavily then on the Mississippi mind as it ever had. Mississippi was still nearly 85 percent rural, and although manufacturing employment had risen somewhat in the 1930s, Mississippi was still wedded to agriculture. No indications appeared that white Mississippians were any more willing to release the black man from economic and social bondage than they had been a century earlier. It was in 1939, after all, that Senator Theodore G. Bilbo introduced into Congress his famous "Greater Liberia Act," a bill providing for the voluntary resettlement of American Negroes in Africa. Then, too, any time that FDR's New Deal hinted, as it inevitably did, at upsetting the racial *status quo,* white Mississippians drew together to defend their racial system. Not coincidentally, Mississippi's most notable (or notorious) modern racist, Theodore Bilbo, gained fame in the 1930s. Bilbo was a good New Dealer consistently supporting, from his senate seat, the president's program of reform—until he realized the impact of the New Deal on race. Like other white Mississippians down the years, when faced with the alternative of economic advancement for all or preservation of the racial *status quo,* he chose the latter.

In the final analysis, the Great Depression and the New Deal brought few basic changes to Mississippi's society or economy. The depression decade only foretold fundamental alterations that would begin in the next decade.

7

Cultural Distinctions

PERHAPS art foretells changes in a society better than political or economic factors, for if the 1930s only hinted at future and fundamental changes in Mississippi's race relations and economy, a few writers of fiction stood then on the brink of world recognition and acclaim. In the 1920s, H. L. Mencken, irascible editor, essayist, and literary critic, had commented, in his usual acid ink, upon "the dreadful literary barrenness of the State of Mississippi." No "printable manuscript," he continued, had ever come from the state, nor had he ever heard of any Mississippian "hatching an idea." [1] Mencken loved hyperbole, but in this instance, not only did he exaggerate—he could not have chosen a less timely occasion to vent his extravagant condemnation.

Certainly one of the most remarkable cultural outpourings in American history has come from the literature of Mississippi in the twentieth century. That some of the greatest fiction in American history came from a place so unexpected—a state so devoid of a literary tradition, so rural, so economically depressed, so educationally bankrupt—is all the more amazing. A state with the wealth and size and urbanity of California or New York would be proud to count among its contributions a William Faulkner or a Eudora Welty, a Richard Wright or a Stark

1. H. L. Mencken, *Prejudices, Fifth Series* (New York: Alfred A. Knopf, 1926), pp. 159–160.

Young, or a Tennessee Williams. For one small rural state to have formed them all is astounding.

No one has ever been able to explain completely this outpouring of great literature from a small and insignificant place in the short span of a generation. There must be some reason other than chance, for, in number and quality, Mississippi writers defy the laws of probability. One reason may be the moral and cultural ambivalence that many Mississippians feel toward their native state. Emotionally, they are imbued with a heritage that they both admire and reject. A love-hate dilemma consciously or unconsciously moved some Mississippi writers to try to explain their heritage. Added to that motive undoubtedly was the fact that Faulkner's generation was caught between two worlds. Throughout Faulkner's work runs the theme of the old (nobility, honor, pride) versus the modern (the cheap, the ambitious, the amoral)—the Sartorises versus the Snopeses. Perhaps Mississippi's writers in the generation before World War II were among the first to see old institutions dying and Mississippi becoming Americanized, a fact perhaps irreversible but not, to them, totally good.

Mississippi's institutions were never picked apart by sociologists, historians, economists, and psychologists. Few essays and academic treatises served to explain Mississippi's past to her own people and the nation. The Faulkners, Wrights, and Youngs then had a fertile field for their art—to explain to us what could not be explained except through art. It is no coincidence that Mississippi's writers have a sense of the past. Of all authors, Faulkner should be a favorite of historians. Historical novelists use the past as a setting. Faulkner uses it as a catalyst. In short, Mississippi authors are trying to understand their own people—to show how the present cannot escape the past. That may not be as self-evident as it first appears, for, as a nation, Americans are increasingly guilty of ignoring the past. In fact, they often reject it.

With supreme poetic neatness, Mississippi claims perhaps the greatest white novelist and the greatest black novelist in American literature—William Faulkner and Richard Wright. Their careers reflect their respective heritages. Faulkner, born in New

Albany and reared at Oxford, left Mississippi reluctantly and only when he needed money. He refused to call himself a literary man, preferring instead to play the role of a country farmer. He bought land, farmed unsuccessfully, and wrote about his own place and his own people. From 1927, when he published his first novel, to the time of his death in 1962, in volume and quality Faulkner's burst of creativity is unequalled in American literature. The names of his greatest books read like an honor roll of modern American novels: *The Sound and the Fury* (1929), *Sartoris* (1929), *As I Lay Dying* (1930), *Sanctuary* (1931), *Light in August* (1932), *Absalom, Absalom!* (1936), *The Unvanquished: Sartoris Stories* (1938), *The Wild Palms* (1939), *The Hamlet* (1940), *Go Down, Moses* (1942), *Intruder in the Dust* (1948), *Knights' Gambit* (1949), *Requiem for a Nun* (1951), *A Fable* (1954), *The Town* (1957), *The Mansion* (1959), and *The Reivers* (1962). In 1949 he won the Nobel Prize.

To read the novels and stories of William Faulkner's Yoknapatawpha saga is to understand Mississippi's history, her people, her guilt, her frustrations, her violence and humor. Literary critics say that Faulkner's genius lies in creating a provincial world in north Mississippi and somehow infusing it with the universal and timeless themes of great literature—ambition, greed, guilt, courage, individuality, a sense of community. They say that Faulkner is understood by all; that his art is relevant, regardless of place and time. No doubt that universality is true. Yet, to imply that Faulkner could as well have fashioned his fictional world microcosm in any provincial place is to limit a chief portion of Faulkner's genius, for his work is not only high art; it is also an explanation of Mississippi. Few Mississippians read Faulkner. Yet, of all people, they should understand his work: in it are their people, their land, and their struggles with themselves.

William Faulkner was born in north Mississippi, and with only temporary forays to Hollywood, New York, and Virginia (mostly to earn money), he lived near the place of his birth, worked there, and died there. He explained his region and its people as only the artist can. The historical forces that have formed (and sometimes haunted) Mississippians are all in his work. Race, with all its burdens of guilt and violence and its genuine affections, lies in such novels as *Light in August* and *Absalom, Absalom!* The Bundrens, in *As I Lay Dying,* share the grinding poverty of Mississippi's hill farmers and their perseverance in the face of defeat. The insularity and pull of the homeland so characteristic of Mississippians is present in Faulkner's characters, from Quentin Compson to V. K. Ratliff to the McCaslins. Faulkner mirrors, too, the moral and emotional ambivalence that haunts many Mississippians. Above all, Faulkner was a moralist. His best people are imbued with courage, the ability to endure, and the independence that Mississippians have always admired and striven to practice. Throughout Faulkner's world there is portrayed a lack of American discipline and organization—a rootedness and haphazardness that drives the more methodical Yankee to distraction.

Faulkner's land is fundamental Mississippi. Yoknapatawpha County is the heartland, a mixture of rich bottoms, gullied red-clay hills, and highlands. At its center is Jefferson, the commercial and governmental community, whose thousand merchants, bankers, county officials, housewives, and laborers serve and depend on the outlying rural areas.

Among Faulkner's people may be found every Mississippian. The Compson and Sartoris families, the rough aristocrats who rule the country, fall, in Faulkner's novels, into an increasingly meaningless existence and lose their grip on the world. They either commit suicide, as Quentin Compson does, or, worse, they join the Snopeses, as does Jason Compson. To replace the declining Compsons rise the Snopeses, a clan of dirt farmers who descend from the hills attached to no motives save ambition, greed, and power. But if Faulkner's people were only planters and rednecks, the picture would be incomplete. The McCaslins are honest, hard-working, sensible yeomen.

Faulkner's land is peopled with as many blacks as whites. They are enduring: Dilsey, the cook, in *Sound and Fury,* is the only binding force left in a disintegrating Compson family. They are cursed: Joe Christmas, in *Light in August,* in doomed by his blackness. Some are gentlemen: Uncle Parsham Hood, in *The Reivers*. Some are proud: Lucas Beauchamp, in

Intruder in the Dust. Always, however, Faulkner's blacks are forced, no matter their circumstances, to play by the white man's rules. In short, all Mississippians are in Faulkner, whether they like it or not. No sensitive Mississippian can read Faulkner without saying to himself, "I know those people."

Faulkner's world develops from a white perspective; the world of Richard Wright reflects the experiences of black Mississippians. Born near Natchez in 1908 and soon deserted by his father, Wright grew up living with his mother and a variety of relatives in Memphis, Tennessee, and Jackson and Greenwood, Mississippi. For Richard Wright, Mississippi was a bitter land, demanding of the blacks nothing less than total submission and spiritual humiliation. He grew up, he said, in a poverty so hopeless that he literally, on occasion, felt near starvation. He lived in a black society largely resigned to its fate. His only contacts with whites produced for him humiliation, degradation, bitterness, and, finally, hatred. Perhaps worse for Wright than his inability to submit was his puzzlement over the caprice of segregation. Often he could not fathom what conduct was expected of the blacks by whites. Hence, oftentimes he committed offense when none was intended. Nor could he understand the seemingly gratuitous brutality meted out by some whites to blacks. One comes to believe that not only could Wright not accept his fate as a black man in Mississippi, he could not even understand its complexities.

An innate independence, dignity, and intelligence made it impossible for him to accept and adapt to a society in which the whites made all the rules. Eventually, he saw only two alternatives for himself. He could submit and lose himself in the pleasures of religion, gambling, drinking, or rationalization, which were allowed the blacks in amused toleration by the whites. These he could not do, so he chose escape. Richard Wright, like thousands of his fellow black Mississippians, became an expatriate. Embittered, without hope of finding dignity in his homeland, Wright left—first to Memphis, then to Chicago—a path taken by thousands of his fellows. Wright's experiences in Chicago, the poverty and wretchedness of ghetto life, proved to him that his problem was not being a Mississippi black, but being an American black. Eventually his bitterness ran so deep that he sought roots and peace in West Africa and Paris. Least of all would he wish Mississippi to claim him. Yet, the bitterness of his art was molded in Mississippi. Of his books, the first three are the most powerful. *Uncle Tom's Children* (1940) consisted of five stories concerning the black condition. In 1940 Wright published his best-known novel, *Native Son,* the story of Bigger Thomas, a young Chicago black man who is so morally and tragically warped by street life in the ghetto that his life ends in execution for murder.

In 1945 appeared Wright's autobiographical *Black Boy,* which treats of the author's own life up to the time he leaves Memphis to migrate to Chicago. It is a powerful and bitter story. Although Wright published later works—*The Outsider* (1953), *Black Power* (1954), *The Color Curtain* (1956), *White Man, Listen* (1957), and *The Long Dream* (1958)—none of them ranked with his first three.

Through Wright's writings runs a torrent of bitterness and rage. Unrelenting as it was in Wright, he had to migrate or be destroyed. Certainly not all Mississippi blacks shared the intensity of Wright's wrath, and surely the races were not separated always as completely as Wright's experience indicates. Yet, with those qualifications, Wright's work speaks not only for black Mississippians, but also for black Americans. Before his death in Paris in 1960, Wright had become so alienated that his work seems weighed down with hate and frustration. Like the characters in his stories, Wright seemed always to be running from his native soil in search of peace. He never found it.

One of America's foremost critics of Southern literature remarked, "In American fiction there are two Mississippis. One is William Faulkner's: a place of violent men and desperate struggle." Faulkner's, he said, was a world of epic proportions, a place of high tragedy, where honor fights baseness and order combats disorder. "The other Mississippi," he continued "is a very different kind of place. . . . a tidy, protected little world," where people go about their daily affairs "in tranquil, pastoral fashion," as if in a dream. "Sometimes the 'real world' peeps in on them, but generally they lock it out, and agree to ignore it.'' [2] This peaceful Mississippi is the country of Eudora Welty—after Wright and Faulkner, Mississippi's most distinguished writer of fiction. Eudora Welty's style is light, deft, conversational, and oblique, almost like the graphic style of a painter of water colors. Her characters do not, on the surface, have purpose or passion; but on closer examination, they do. It is almost as if Miss Welty's characters are all engaged in a conspiracy to keep the real world of passions, dangers, chaos, from intruding, while they fill their days with visitings, weddings, funerals, and meals. She has the eye of an artist and the ear of a musician, for she captures the daily living of small-town Mississippians perfectly.

Her writings are as funny as Faulkner's. Where Faulkner's humor is raucous and frontierlike, Miss Welty's is subtle, sneaking up on the reader through the foibles, eccentricities, and conversations of her characters.

Perhaps the strongest characteristic of Eudora Welty's work—and she shares this with Faulkner—is the strong sense of community and family that flows through her short stories and novels. At a time when the new urban Americans not only have no roots or neighbors but no homes, perhaps Eudora Welty's and William Faulkner's ultimate appeal is that they write about people wedded to place.

One of the finest autobiographies ever written by a Southerner was published in 1940 by Greenville poet-planter-community leader William Alexander Percy. He remembered the guards who marched on the levees along the Mississippi River in the Delta, guarding against breaks or sabotage of the Mississippi side by Arkansans who wanted to relieve pressure on their side. The guards carried lanterns and guns. Percy called his book *Lanterns on the Levee*. Will Percy was the son of Leroy Percy, United States senator, lawyer, and wealthy planter. If the Delta had an aristocracy, the Percys stood at its head. *Lanterns on the Levee,* more than a simple autobiography, is an autobiographical lament for the passing of an old, honorable, pleasant

2. Louis D. Rubin, Jr., *The Faraway Country: Writers of the Modern South* (Seattle: University of Washington Press, 1963), pp. 131–132.

life, in which affairs were determined by *noblesse oblige,* and the modern rise of the cheap, ambitious, and shallow. *Lanterns on the Levee* is the Faulknerian Sartoris-versus-Snopes in autobiographical form.

In 1934 Stark Young wrote *So Red the Rose,* a romantic novel of Natchez and the Civil War. The book draws the impact of secession and war on two great Natchez plantation families. Even though they opposed secession, the great planters suffered most from the South's defeat; they had the greatest distance to fall. Young makes that point well, perhaps better than the more famous but similar *Gone With The Wind,* which was published by Margaret Mitchell of Georgia a few years afterwards.

Mississippi has produced many other good authors. To list them would be a difficult task. Many chose to live outside Mississippi but have roots in the state—Tennessee Williams, Walker Percy (William Alexander's nephew), Shelby Foote, whose early novels are overshadowed by his monumental three-volume history, *The Civil War.* No state, however populous, has furnished the nation more great literature than Mississippi. Finally, Mississippians may realize, as many other Americans already do, that the state's greatest gift to the nation has been cultural, not political or economic or social.

Hardly as famous, but perhaps as influential, were the sometimes mournful, oftentimes happy sounds of the blues. Mississippians grew up with the blues as background music and hardly noticed it. As a child before World War II, this writer spent some summers with his grandparents in Delta City, a crossroads hamlet in Sharkey County surrounded on all sides by great cotton fields. On Saturdays, my cousin and I usually wandered up the gravel road across the Dump (an old railroad right-of-way with the tracks removed to convert it into a sort of elevated road). Five stores clustered around the crossroads; we always mounted the open-board steps, crossed the porch, where wooden benches formed banisters, and went through the screened double doors into a long barnlike frame store called Chatney's. There we would hang around, two eight-year-old white faces drinking strawberry soda and eating ice cream in a sea of rural Delta blacks who liked strawberry soda and ice cream as much as we did. Chatney's was a country store primarily for the black trade. Mr. Chatney's stock included big felt hats with long colored feathers, pegged pants for dress, straw hats, overalls, and clodhoppers for work shoes. Just inside the door stood a fat, brightly-colored juke box. It fascinated us, with its bubbles running up and down the sides in little tubes. Out of it poured unintelligible, mournful wails that most whites disdainfully called "Negro music." Fifteen years later, in a post exchange in Heidelberg, I bought a record, mainly because it was on sale and because it had been recorded by a fellow Mississippian—Big Bill Broonzy, a blues singer from Scott, Mississippi, who in the 1950s was more famous in Europe than in America. Broonzy's music was identical to that I had heard at Chatney's Store. I then realized that, under our noses in the rural Mississippi Delta, a musical revolution had arisen to sweep the United States and even Europe.

The blues were born in the Mississippi Delta before World War I. Nobody is certain where the name came from, or what it means, beyond the fact that it obviously describes troubles—usually with women, the law, the landlord, whiskey, cotton, or money. The blues apparently developed almost spontaneously, a synthesis of the "field hollers"—long, rhythmic discourses that field hands repeated when chopping or picking—and Negro spirituals. One of the most influential Mississippi blues men was Charles Patton. Born about 1885 near Edwards, Mississippi, Patton's parents moved their twelve children, around 1900, to a large plantation called Dockery's, in Sunflower County. There Patton stayed until he was thirty-four. The origins of his musical talents are obscure, but by the time he left Dockery's, he was accomplished enough to team up with a fiddle-player named Son Sims, play the jukes, and record for Paramount Records. Even before he left Dockery's, Patton had become both a teacher and a hero to other aspiring Negro blues singers, and his disciples multiplied with astonishing speed.

Mississippi Delta blues between World Wars I and II became the model, the standard by which other blues music was measured. Whatever its origins, blues became the central music of

Mississippi's peasantry, sung in the black "jukes" along every highway and dirt road in the Delta. The blues accompanied good times and bad Saturday-night cuttings, shootings, and scrapes with the law. Finally, by World War II, the blues formed a major source for all American popular music, from jazz to contemporary country. Few Mississippians have heard of Charley Patton or Son House or Honeyboy Johnson or Bo Carter or the influence of Dockery's Plantation on American music. That does not alter the fact that, notwithstanding such great classical musicians as Leontyne Price of Laurel and composer William Grant Still from Wilkinson County, Mississippi's greatest musical contribution may be the music of Delta sharecroppers. And one of Mississippi's chief legacies to America may be music.

8

Change and Continuity: Since 1945

MISSISSIPPI prepared to enter the greatest war effort in American history with institutions rooted in 1840. From 1840, when the state's basic institutions emerged, down to 1940, when some indications of change began to appear, the historian is struck more by how much alike the eras were than by their differences, more by the continuity of Mississippi's institutions than by the change. Mississippi's writers in the 1930s and 1940s were among the first to see that a new, more American Mississippi stood on the horizon, and, conversely, that the old, familiar characteristics were doomed. Like William Faulkner's Snopeses who displaced the aristocratic Sartoris family, the new era would be fascinating and energetic, but materialistic and ambitious.

The beginning of the end for the old order that had prevailed since the 1840s came with the Second World War. It is too great a claim to say that World War II *caused* the agricultural, industrial, and demographic revolutions that occurred in the generation after 1945. Yet it is not too much to claim that the

The material in this chapter dealing with World War II first appeared in an article by the author entitled "World War II as a Watershed in Mississippi History," *The Journal of Mississippi History* 37 (1975): 135–141. It is reprinted here by permission of the Mississippi Historical Society.

Second World War was a watershed for Mississippi, a convenient and readily identifiable era, before which there was basic historical continuity for a century, but after which nothing ever again was quite the same. Much of the change that World War II brought to Mississippi seemed momentary and appeared to recede as soon as the war ended. The army camps, the boom towns of Pascagoula, Biloxi, and Hattiesburg, and even much of the prosperity seemed after 1945 to be gone with the war. But the taste lingered, and the results lasted. Nearly a quarter of a million Mississippians entered the armed forces during the war, and at least as many non-Mississippians became temporary residents, either at training camps or in some other wartime capacity. Many in both groups had their illusions shattered. Mississippians could hardly come home with the same provincial and insulated attitudes, after traveling over the United States and overseas. In short, Mississippians during the war were introduced to the country, and the country discovered Mississippi, and, psychologically, things could never be the same. The foregoing is admittedly subjective and difficult to quantify. There is, however, some objective data to support the thesis that World War II was a watershed in Mississippi history.

Mississippians tasted prosperity during the war years. Per-capita income rose between 1941 and 1945 from $313 to $627, from 44 percent of the national average to slightly more than 50 percent in 1945. Total income payments increased from $88 million in 1942 to $1.224 billion in 1945. Demand deposits in banks grew during the same period from just over $148 million to almost $672 million. By 1944 another $111 million dollars was in savings bonds. Not only were more Mississippians making and saving more money than ever before, but also they began, in the war years, to retire their debts. During the same period, when income and savings were rising dramatically, farm mortgages declined from $102 million dollars to $83 million. During the war years, Mississippians enjoyed an affluence undreamed of only months earlier, and they liked it. In the postwar years, hardly a politician could be elected who did not include as major planks in his platform a dedication to industrialization and a rise in personal income.

New trends were established in agriculture during the years of the Second World War. Between 1940 and 1945, farm population declined 26 percent. During the same period, the number of farms declined almost 10 percent, the sharpest drop in the South. At the same time, total farm acreage rose slightly, as did the average farm size. Farm tenancy was dealt a blow during the years of the war when 30 percent of all white tenants and 14 percent of all black tenants left the farm. Most of these migrants were in the age group below thirty-five.

Mississippians moved about during World War II in greater numbers than at any time since the Civil War. More than 237,000 citizens served in the armed forces during the years of the war. Of that number, more than 60,000 were no longer citizens of the state in 1947. Out-migration during the 1940s was great. Net out-migration during the decade totaled almost 400,000. Approximately 75 percent of those were black.

Evidence indicates that a dramatic reshuffling of Mississippi's population began in the 1940s. The preponderance of blacks in the population dropped significantly. Tremendous out-migration of blacks to such states of the North as Michigan and Illinois occurred. Whites moved at a lesser rate to the bordering states of Tennessee, Alabama, and Louisiana. Although movement from rural areas accelerated, the fastest-growing segment of the population soon came to be the rural nonfarm category, workers who lived in the country but earned their money in town. Population shifts within the state favored Hinds County and the Gulf Coast. Such great mobility reduced provincialism and changed values.

The issue of race, relatively dormant for three decades, surfaced during World War II. The issue would explode after the war, cutting Mississippi's nearly century-old allegiance to the Democratic party and dominating the mind of the state for the next twenty years. The war years produced a number of issues—some legitimate and some specious—that centered the attention of Mississippians on race and the attention of the nation on Mississippi.

On June 25, 1941, President Franklin Roosevelt published Executive Order 8802, banning discrimination in war industries and establishing a Fair Employment Practices Committee to "receive and investigate complaints of discrimination, to implement the order." The first FEPC had little success. On May 27, 1943, FDR created a new and more independent committee, subject directly to him.

Two Mississippi congressmen, Senator Theodore G. Bilbo and Congressman John Rankin, gained national notoriety from their opposition to FEPC. Bilbo charged that "every Negro in America who is behind movements of this kind . . . dream[s] of social equality and inter-marriage between whites and blacks." Rankin called the FEPC "the beginning of a Communistic dictatorship, the like of which America never dreamed." [1]

Perhaps a more sensitive issue even than the FEPC was the prospect in late 1943 and early 1944 that FDR and many in Congress wished to exercise federal power to assist absentee balloting by soldiers. Late in 1943, legislation was introduced into Congress providing for an absentee voting law for servicemen. The administration bill called for a federal ballot and federally controlled qualifications for absentee voters. Obviously, in the eyes of Southern congressmen, this held the possibility for great evil—the prospect of uncontrolled black voting. From December 1943 to February 1944, arguments grew more heated between the administration and its supporters and a coalition of Southern congressmen and their conservative Republican allies. The Southerners favored state ballots and state voter qualifications. Led by Senator James O. Eastland in the Senate and John Rankin in the House, the states'-righters ultimately won when Congress approved a bill that allowed the states to provide their own ballots and judge the qualifications of the soldiers who cast them.

The fight attracted attention in the state press. In support of Eastland's stand against a federally controlled absentee ballot for soldiers, the *Jackson Clarion-Ledger* remarked editorially that Mississippi soldiers would "much rather lose their chance to vote in one or two elections . . . than for their state to lose

1. Louis Ruchames, *Race, Jobs, and Politics: The Story of FEPC* (New York: Columbia University Press, 1953), pp. 94, 98.

control of voting requirements and qualifications. They know what loss of such control would mean."[2] Running for re-election to the United States Senate in 1946, Theodore Bilbo painted for the white voters of Mississippi fearful pictures of masses of Negro veterans flocking to the polls to vote in a bloc. To forestall such a possibility, the Mississippi legislature soon after the war revised the state's primary election laws to make it harder for blacks to qualify.

Other evidence that the old racial fears were reviving during the war may be found in the number and diversity of rumors that swept the state. Housewives whispered that Eleanor Roosevelt was sponsoring the organization of "Eleanor Clubs" among black women to "put a white woman in every kitchen." Such a rumor was easy for some to believe, because many black women could receive higher wages in the war economy than they could as cooks and maids. No Eleanor Clubs were ever discovered. Other even less believable rumors had Negroes arming themselves with ice picks to use in an uprising, or arming themselves with guns and ammunition for the same purpose, or planning to take over at home while many white men were away in the armed forces, or planning uprisings by Negro veterans after the war.

These rumors seem hardly credible today, but they indicate that the war years did produce much racial fear and tension and set into motion what some historians have called "the second Reconstruction"—one whose effects may be more long-lasting than the first.

Strains appeared also in Mississippi's long allegiance to the Democratic party. Both candidates in the 1943 gubernatorial run-off, Mike Conner and Tom Bailey, criticized the growing bureaucracy in Washington and emphasized states' rights. A surprise coup in the 1944 state democratic convention gave momentary control of the convention to anti-FDR forces, and a slate of anti-New Deal electors was chosen. Only after last-minute maneuvering and a special session of the legislature was the mini-revolt crushed. Mississippi's voters overwhelmingly

2. *Jackson Clarion-Ledger,* January 26, 1944.

endorsed FDR for a fourth term and repudiated the anti-FDR forces, but as the author of the story of that unsuccessful revolt states, there may be

> a thin link between the Mississippi elections of 1944 and 1948. The fact that in nine of the heavily Negro populated counties, the "Bolters" in 1944 received their highest percentage of the Democratic vote indicates that the seeds of discontent based on the race issue had been sown. In this light the election of 1944 appears to be the "crack in the dam" which would burst and overflow four years later.[3]

So by 1945 Mississippians were on notice that their economic, social, political, and racial institutions would not be, in the future, what they had been in the past.

The process of change tentatively begun in Mississippi by the war afterwards gathered speed. In the three decades following the Second World War, every one of the peculiar characteristics that had dominated Mississippi during the previous century disintegrated, either under external pressure or from internal desires for change. Between 1945 and 1975, revolutions occurred in agriculture, industry, demography, income, and, most important of all, race—revolutions that brought an end to sharecropping and Jim Crowism, to the hegemony of King Cotton, to Mississippi's isolation from the nation. As the old institutions decayed, alongside arose a society and economy not unlike the American dream: affluence and urbanization, industry and agricultural diversity, and—albeit after much prodding and pushing—political and economic opportunity for the black man.

Of course it is in the realm of race that Mississippians received most national attention after World War II. The conflicts between black and white, between state and federal authority, certainly are the most visible issues in Mississippi history since the Second World War. The history of Mississippi's postwar wrestlings with race came in two waves—from 1945 to 1964, defiance of the national will; after 1964, acquiescence.

Mississippi, despite some tensions, emerged from World War

3. Roy H. Ruby, "The Presidential Election of 1944 in Mississippi: The Bolting Electors" (M.A. thesis, Mississippi State University, 1966), pp. 49–50.

II with her peculiar racial customs intact. Hardly did the veterans have time to doff their uniforms before the race issue, relatively dormant since the days of Vardaman, re-emerged. Apparently afraid that returning Negro veterans had developed ideas of political independence while away at war, white Mississippians prepared for an onslaught of black voters. Governor Fielding L. Wright in 1947 called a special session of the legislature to strengthen Mississippi's defenses by adding new voter laws. The white primary had been outlawed by the United States Supreme Court in 1944, so the legislators felt it necessary to protect the ballot box by empowering county election officials to challenge voters. So that the officials would know whom to challenge, the lawmakers added, "Any person who has participated in three primary elections . . . shall not be subject to challenge." [4]

A year earlier, in 1946, Senator Theodore G. Bilbo had reached new heights of racial demagoguery in his campaign for a third term in the United States Senate. That campaign showed clearly that the old racial fears had not died, and the aftermath of the election showed that the old sense of isolation and persecution still thrived. In the election of 1946, Bilbo defeated four opponents in the first Democratic primary, but he did so by appealing to the fears of Mississippi voters in the most blatant use of the race question since Vardaman's 1903 campaign. He called upon white Mississippians to use "any means" to keep Negroes from the polls. More specifically, he commanded, "I am calling upon every red-blooded American who believes in the superiority and integrity of the white race to get out and see that no nigger votes . . . and the best time to do it is the night before." [5] Bilbo spiced his inflammatory campaign speeches with occasional obscene references to Clare Booth Luce and Eleanor Roosevelt, whom he branded as promoters of Negro equality and to the supposed savagery of the black man, who, according to Bilbo, was "only 150 years removed from Africa

4. *Laws of Mississippi, 1947,* p. 22.

5. *United States Senate Reports, 80th Congress, 1st session* (Washington: Government Printing Office, 1947), p. 14.

where it was his great delight to cut him up some fried nigger steak for breakfast.''[6]

For his conduct in the 1946 campaign, Bilbo was charged with intimidating Negro voters. Investigated by his senatorial colleagues, Bilbo was exonerated on a strict partisan vote. But he was not to survive another set of charges. Before he appeared to take his seat for the 1947 session, Bilbo was accused by the Congressional War Investigating Committee of receiving wartime bribes from contractors. He faced the third bribery scandal of his career. An effort was made, at the opening of the 1947 Congress, to deny Bilbo his seat. At the height of the controversy, sick and apparently afraid he would lose, Bilbo left Washington for New Orleans. At Ochsner Clinic, he underwent surgery for cancer. Bilbo never returned to renew the fight for his seat in the Senate. He died on August 21, 1947—ironically, from cancer of the mouth.

Bilbo's last battle proved Mississippi's sense of persecution still persisted. In the campaign of 1946, many national publications had advised Mississippi not to return Bilbo to the United States Senate. As a result, many a Mississippian who had never supported "The Man" "held his nose and voted for Bilbo."[7] In addition, Bilbo became to white Mississippians a sort of racist martyr—one who had been done in by the hated neo-abolitionists. His racial beliefs became gospel to the segregationists of the 1950s and 1960s who inherited his mantle. The segregationist liturgy went something like this: economic equality leads to political equality; both will produce social equality, which, in turn, will lead to miscegenation—the ultimate dread. Physical separation of the races furnished the only hope of protecting white purity. Bilbo sounded these warnings in his book *Take Your Choice: Separation or Mongrelization,* published shortly before his death in 1947.

If the events of 1946 and 1947 indicated that white Mississippians would not relinquish their racial institutions without a

6. *United States Senate Reports, 80th Congress, 1st session,* p. 21.

7. V. O. Key, Jr., *Southern Politics in State and Nation* (New York: Alfred A. Knopf, 1949), p. 244.

struggle, 1948 proved that they would even abandon the Democratic party to save segregation. After the party nominated Harry Truman and endorsed a platform calling for an end to racial discrimination, Mississippians, led by Governor Fielding L. Wright, seceded from the party. The state denied its vote to the Democrats for the first time since Reconstruction and voted instead for the Dixiecrat Ticket of Strom Thurmond and Fielding Wright. Hoping to show the party that it could not win without support of the white South, the Dixiecrats proved just the opposite, for Truman won without the votes of Mississippi, South Carolina, Alabama, and Louisiana. Mississippi would not vote for a winning presidential candidate again until 1972, when Republican Richard Nixon won the state's electoral votes.

In 1954, when the United States Supreme Court handed down the *Brown* decision outlawing segregation in the public schools, white Mississippians first reacted with shock. Upon reflection, however, many concluded that there was little to fear, for, they said, true Mississippians would neither tolerate the decision nor obey it. Fred Sullens, editor of the *Jackson Daily News* and Mississippi's most widely read journalist, seemed to speak for many white Mississippians when he called the decision a "calamity" and prophesied bloodshed—blood that would stain the steps of the Supreme Court building. Mississippians, he predicted, would not obey the ruling, and if legal evasions proved fruitless, violence would follow.

From 1955 to 1960, Mississippians mobilized their defenses, both legal and extralegal, against integration. The legislature prepared new laws and repealed old ones, hoping so to entangle the adversary in legal barbed wire that the issue could be postponed indefinitely. Into the code went laws permitting the abolition of public schools, upholding the validity of the antiquated doctrine of interposition—an antebellum doctrine that held that the sovereignty of a state could be interposed between federal law and the people. Other bills established a State Sovereignty Commission to protect the state from encroachments of federal power, allowed tuition grants to students attending private schools, attempted to curb civil rights suits, and discouraged out-of-state lawyers from practicing before Mississippi courts.

Out of the code came Mississippi's compulsory school attendance law, and the voters repealed the portion of the state constitution requiring public schools.

Soon after the *Brown* decision, a new, extralegal shadow government arose in Mississippi. The White Citizens' Councils, born at Indianola and destined to blanket the state by 1960, were dedicated both to perpetuating racial orthodoxy and to spreading the word in the northern and western states that all Mississippians, white and black, were satisfied with the racial *status quo*. The councils were dedicated, first, to insuring the unity of white Mississippians and next to insuring that Mississippi blacks remained quiet and nonmilitant. Consisting mostly of urban, middle-class business and professional men, the councils renounced violence, preferring to enforce the orthodoxy through economic pressure, political intimidation, social ostracism, and a vigorous propaganda campaign dedicated to the idea that "if you're not with us, you're against us."

From 1959 to 1964, while Ross Barnett was governor of Mississippi, the Citizens' Councils achieved unprecedented power. With offices just across the street from the governor's mansion, council chieftan William J. Simmons advised legislators, consulted almost daily with Governor Ross Barnett, organized schools, sent speakers northward to carry the segregationist message, policed textbooks, and generally protected the citizens of the state from integrationists—both "outside agitators" and those few natives who braved the segregationist conformity that by 1960 pervaded white Mississippi.

Yet, as Mississippi seemed most unyielding in her defense of the old racial ways, events were converging that in a very short time would crush segregationist resistance and, almost overnight, create incredible racial change. The years from 1962 through 1964 were pivotal in the history of Mississippi race relations. During those months, resistance to racial change by white Mississippians reached its zenith and almost simultaneously started to recede, producing from 1965 forward an almost complete crumbling of the old racial order.

By 1962 Mississippians lived as nearly under an enforced orthodoxy as have any Americans. In the minds of the white majority had arisen a kind of neo-secessionism. The white Citizens' Councils became the enforcers of a common set of ideas and rationalizations concerning race and the federal government that few outsiders could comprehend. Common words and phrases took on new and special meanings: "our Southern way of life" meant segregation; anyone questioning "our Southern way of life" was "communistic," whether or not he had the slightest familiarity with the writings of Karl Marx. "Moderate" described anyone with doubts about the orthodoxy as defined by the Citizens' Councils. One political figure was described as "a moderate of the worst sort." The press of the state, led by the Jackson papers, the *Daily News* and the *Clarion-Ledger,* formed powerful organs for the orthodoxy. Only in a few cities—Greenville, McComb, Tupelo, Pascagoula—did the newspapers remain independent and unintimidated by the defenders of the racial *status quo.* By 1962 lines were drawn clearly. Consciously, the Citizens' Councils attempted to force Mississippians from the middle ground. Time and again they drummed the litany: "You are either for segregation or against it." Segregation was equated with God, free enterprise, and—strangely—freedom and individual liberty. Those who defended it were "patriotic." Those who attacked it were "communists" and potential "tyrants." The federal government was the enemy. The councils enforced the orthodoxy by economic pressure, threats of social ostracism, and the simple desire of many Mississippians to be liked—to be a part of the community. Most natives with doubts about the orthodoxy stayed silent or left the state. Political leaders either accepted the orthodoxy or were forced into alignment.

Ross Barnett, elected Governor of Mississippi on his fourth attempt, was the man destined to lead Mississippi through the crucial months of 1962 to 1963. An engaging and genial man, Barnett was not a classic racial demagogue in the Bilbo-Vardaman tradition, nor did he share their economic and political progressivism. In his economic and political views, Barnett resembled the conservative "Redeemers" who governed Mississippi in the late nineteenth century. By 1959 he was a rich damage-suit lawyer who wished to cap his successful law career with the honor of being governor. Friendly with large business interests—utilities, railroads, trucking firms, and bankers—his two great dreams were to bring industry and economic development to Mississippi and to maintain the racial *status quo*. Apparently, he failed to see that his goals were antithetical—that so long as the black man remained poor, so would most whites. Governor Barnett, as later events would prove, was not a very hateable political leader, even by those who disagreed with him. Barnett never controlled events, even in the bitter and violence-ridden months of 1962–1963. Events and other men controlled him. Naive, pliable, eager to please his constituency, and obsessed with his image, Barnett was swept along by events he hardly understood, caught between dedicated forces who knew exactly what they wanted—the Citizens' Councils on one side and the civil rights movement on the other.

Inevitably, the final confrontation between the forces of change and those who supported the *status quo* approached. By 1962 many white Mississippians had developed the mentality of a people beseiged by federal power that wished to wipe out Mississippi's peculiar racial customs. Years of bitter and divisive rhetoric almost insured that the confrontation would be violent. "An all-out war is being waged against the white race," [8] wrote council leader Simmons. Almost all political leaders parroted the council line. Moderate views were either silenced or laughingly tolerated. Mississippi's modern Armageddon began with the violence at Ole Miss surrounding the admission of James Meredith in 1962 and ended in the long, hot summer of 1964 with the murder of three young civil rights workers in Neshoba County—events that brought Mississippi to the brink of insurrection. Mississippi in the national mind became synonymous with stubborn resistance to civil rights, with night-riding violence and intimidation, with the cry "never" to integration.

In that climate, a twenty-eight-year-old Air Force veteran from Jackson State College applied to enter the University of Mississippi. James Howard Meredith had been born and reared

8. W. J. Simmons, "Organization: Key to Victory," *The Citizen* 6 (February 1962): 7.

in Attala County, in the red-clay hills of central Mississippi. Even in high school, Meredith showed a great sensitivity to segregation. Partly to escape his second-class citizenship, Meredith, after spending his last high-school year in Florida, joined the Air Force. He served nine years before returning to his home state in 1960. While in the Air Force, Meredith accumulated a number of college credits, and he came home with the plan to finish his degree in two years. But where to go? Meredith chose Jackson State, Mississippi's largest and liveliest black college. At Jackson State, Meredith, who stoutly maintained that he wanted nothing more than the best education the state could furnish, determined to transfer to the University of Mississippi. In 1961, when Meredith wrote the registrar at Ole Miss for application forms, no black attended any public educational institution in Mississippi, and Governor Ross Barnett assured Mississippi's white citizens that so long as he was governor, none would. Indeed, two earlier abortive attempts had been made to integrate Mississippi's public colleges. Clennon King in 1958 was committed to the state mental hospital after trying to enroll at Ole Miss, and Clyde Kennard was denied admission to Mississippi Southern College after his conviction for stealing three sacks of chicken feed—a crime for which he was sentenced to seven years in the state penitentiary. Rumors circulated that Kennard had been framed.

Meredith determined to try, anyway. He solicited support from Medgar Evers, state secretary for the National Association for the Advancement of Colored People and himself later to be a martyr to the civil rights cause in 1963. Meredith needed help, for it took sixteen months of hearings, appeals, injunctions, contempt citations, a full-scale riot costing two lives, great property damage and thousands of federal troops to overcome the stubborn resistance of two centuries of Mississippi history. Even after his admission on September 30, 1962, Meredith had to be guarded by soldiers and United States marshals for the entire year that he remained at the university. Students not only harassed Meredith, but threatened and ostracized any white students who showed sympathy for him. Frustrated, Meredith once referred to himself as the most segregated black in the world.

Despite the shootings, rioting, and threats of violence that had attended his admission, Meredith stayed on to graduate. Only nine months after Meredith's admission, Medgar Evers, who had pledged the resources of the NAACP to Meredith's cause, himself was shot in the back from ambush as he stepped from his car in his own driveway. The FBI worked quickly to arrest Byron de La Beckwith, a fertilizer salesman from Greenwood. Beckwith was tried twice, but both prosecutions ended in mistrials when the juries could not agree on a verdict. Medgar Evers was not the only man to be killed in the cause of black civil rights, but he was certainly the most well-known. His assassination brought Mississippi's national image to a new low.

Precisely a year later, still greater violence brought even worse notoriety. The summer of 1964 brought hundreds of young college students to Mississippi. Their aim was to uplift the black man, to awaken Mississippi blacks to their second-class citizenship and to do battle with Jim Crow. Under the leadership of civil rights organizations like the Student Non-Violent Coordinating Committee, Congress of Racial Equality, and the Southern Christian Leadership Conference, the students worked in "freedom schools" and voter registration drives. They were energetic, aggressive, idealistic, and some said naive. If indeed they were naive, their innocence was soon shattered, for in June 1964 three of their number—Michael Schwerner, James Chaney, and Andrew Goodman—were seized and shot to death. Some Mississippians stoutly maintained that they had been spirited from the state by their own colleagues to create propaganda for the civil rights cause. After an intensive search their bodies were uncovered in an earthen dam. Eventually a number of Ku Klux Klansmen went to federal prison for "violating the civil rights" of Schwerner, Chaney, and Goodman. Out of this "Freedom Summer" emerged a dedicated—and, considering the stubborn reluctance of white Mississippians to give up their old racial habits, a restrained—black leadership: Aaron Henry, president of the state NAACP; Charles Evers, brother of Medgar and field secretary of the NAACP; Fannie Lou Hamer and Lawrence Guyot, of the Student Nonviolent Coordinating Committee.

Even as white Mississippi appeared most unyielding in 1963 and 1964, resistance, in fact, was on the threshold of collapse. When Mississippi's old racial system came down, it crumbled with a suddenness and a rush that surprised whites, blacks, Mississippians, and non-Mississippians.

The collapse occurred and the change came for a variety of reasons. Moderates and even many sincere segregationists were shocked by the violence. The Ole Miss riot and its aftermath proved to many that there were extremist forces in the state whose main interest was not, as they claimed, in preserving the racial *status quo,* but in destruction. These extremists horrified Ole Miss alumni when they pressured Governor Barnett to close the university. They believed, apparently, that destroying a century-old university and sending home a few thousand students was not too great a price to pay to keep out one black. Other Mississippians did not agree. Then, too, few Mississippians before 1962 thought that resistance would entail cold-blooded assassinations—a black leader shot in the back from ambush in 1963 and three young men kidnapped and executed in 1964. Violence and even murder had occurred earlier, and some would come afterwards, but the killing of Evers, Goodman, Chaney, and Schwerner proved pivotal in mobilizing moderate reaction in Mississippi. Ultimately, the last-ditch segregationists who promoted or condoned violence were done in by their own excesses, for they began to mobilize the moderates—whites largely silent until 1964 who believed that the state should bow gracefully to integration and black voting.

One would like to conclude that moral outrage was enough to turn the tide. Yet, as important as that was, another factor was more crucial: the economic consequences of continued resistance, violence, and a bad press. Among the first to speak out for an end to resistance, to call for coolness and moderation, were business leaders. Early in 1965, both the Mississippi Economic Council and the Mississippi Manufacturers Association adopted resolutions endorsing an end to violence and the recognition by Mississippians that they could not indefinitely encourage defiance. Then, too, national businesses with outlets in Mississippi—motels, restaurants, concerns catering to the public—found it increasingly hard to justify their acceptance of local segregationist customs. The public-accommodations section of the Civil Rights Act of 1964 came as a relief to many businessmen who could now say to the diehards, "We must obey the law." Nor could Mississippi, a state whose citizens received three dollars from Washington for every one they paid in, ignore threats from Washington to cut off federal funds. As the state's racial climate threatened to discourage economic expansion, Mississippians took notice and, for the first time, recognized, as one controversial professor put it, that "a healthy modern industrial structure cannot be raised upon the sands of segregation, minimum wages, poor schools, anti-unionism, and a general policy of 'hate the federal government.' "[9]

For the first time, too, a leading political leader spoke out in favor of rejoining the union. Governor Paul B. Johnson served as lieutenant governor during the Meredith crisis. On one occasion, when Governor Barnett's plane was delayed, it was Johnson who turned Meredith and Chief Marshal James McShane away from the gate at Ole Miss. Johnson had run for governor without success in three previous campaigns. His well-publicized shoving match with McShane made him Barnett's successor. Running on the slogan "Stand Tall with Paul," Johnson in 1963 won the governorship after a race-baiting campaign that would have done credit to Vardaman or Bilbo. But Johnson was no Barnett. From the time of his inauguration, Johnson showed himself a man who wished to calm passions, not inflame them, a man who understood that economic development could only occur in a climate of good will. "I would point out to you," he said in his 1964 inaugural, "that the Mississippi economy is not divisible by political party or faction, or even by race, color, or creed. . . . I will say to you," he continued, "that you and I are a part of this world, whether we like it or not. . . . Too, we are Americans as well as Mississippians. . . . We are at this moment 'in the mainstream of national life.' National policies have a direct bearing on our econ-

9. James W. Silver, *Mississippi: The Closed Society* (New York: Harcourt Brace and World, Inc., 1964), p. 77.

omy, on our political freedom, on our daily living, whether we like it or not." [10]

So, ultimately, the economic argument cut most convincingly among Mississippi's leaders; they finally realized, after 1964, that the state would remain in the economic backwaters as long as it retained the old racial ways. Finally real change came. Racial peace settled over the state in the 1970s. Mississippi's public schools survived and now are among the most integrated in America. The battleground of race shifted northward. After such a long and bitter struggle with themselves, Mississippians now must be forgiven if they occasionally smile smugly at Boston or Detroit, the principal scenes of racial confrontation in the mid-1970s.

Although the violent conflicts that attended Mississippi's abandonment of the racial *status quo* have received the most national attention, since the Second World War the old Mississippi has been remade in other quieter revolutions. The demographic patterns that emerged in Mississippi in the generation after World War II are in most cases reversals of century-old patterns. Mississippi's total population has remained all but unchanged since 1940, but within that stable framework a number of startling new departures became increasingly apparent.

Nobody has fully examined the impact on Mississippi's changing race relations of the changing ratio of blacks to whites. One suspects that it is very important. Typically, in modern times, the state of Mississippi has had the highest ratio of blacks to whites of any state in the nation—by 1900, three blacks for every two whites. Seventy years later, the census of 1970 showed Mississippi's population to be only 37 percent black and 63 percent white. Among the great untold stories of American history is that of the mass exodus since World War II of Southern blacks to the industrial cities of the North and the East. In fact, two great black migrations begun in the First World War have accelerated since 1940—out-migration up the Illinois Central Railroad by Mississippi blacks bound for Chicago, Detroit, Milwaukee, and Gary. At the same time, as agri-

10. *Mississippi Senate Journal,* 1964, pp. 37–38.

cultural diversification and mechanization killed tenancy, rural blacks moved to Mississippi's cities. Hence Mississippi's cities are increasingly black, while the rural population is increasingly white.

Other population changes, if not as critical for the race question, nevertheless are important reversals of past trends. As late as 1940, Mississippi's people were 80 percent rural, down from a high of 98.2 percent in 1850. Mississippi, contrary to popular belief, is still a rural state, though significantly less so than in previous decades. The census of 1970 shows that 55 percent of Mississippians live in the country. Mississippi is nearly twice as rural as the nation. Yet these figures hardly reflect the true dimensions of change in the urban-rural readjustments.

In north Mississippi, nearly every small town has its garment factory. The surrounding countryside is filled with "go-getters"—country men who take their wives to work at the garment plant in the mornings and go get them in the evening. The fastest-growing group in Mississippi's population is the rural nonfarmer. He lives in the country, while he earns his livelihood in town. The rural nonfarm group in the 1950 census numbered slightly more than one-fifth of all Mississippians. By 1960 they numbered 37.4 percent, almost equaling the state's urban population. In 1970 the rural nonfarm inhabitants comprised 43.5 percent of Mississippi's population. It is no accident that the pickup truck has become the badge of the rural nonfarmer. He lives on what at one time was a family farm, but his principal earnings come from his job in town. Though he is not dependent on his land for livelihood, he almost certainly raises vegetables and a few cattle. His is not an unenviable life. He has combined the advantages of country life with some urban affluence. As Mississippians abandon their old living patterns, they are not in all respects exchanging them, helter-skelter, for the kind of urbanized, industrialized life that other Americans must now recognize as a mixed blessing.

Perhaps the most dramatic change of all has been the cluster of changes affecting Mississippi agriculture. For two hundred years almost the sole provider in Mississippi's economy, agriculture no longer occupies such a central place in Mississippi's economic system. It is no longer the chief employer nor the chief income-producer for Mississippians. Although by 1974 more than four times as many Mississippians were employed in agriculture as in the United States as a whole (22 percent in Mississippi, 5 percent nationally), manufacturing employment in Mississippi was both greater than agricultural employment and slightly higher than manufacturing nationally (24.5 percent for Mississippi, 24.2 percent nationally).

As dramatic as the loss of agricultural primacy in Mississippi's economy were the changes that took place within Mississippi's agricultural sector in the last generation. Tenancy disappeared. Between 1940 and 1970, the number of farms in the state declined by 75 percent, while the size of the average farm nearly tripled. Those who remained on farms in Mississippi became more prosperous. In 1951 the net income for a Mississippi farmer was about half the national average for farmers. By 1972 a Mississippi farmer could expect to earn 90 percent of the national average income for farmers. The rise of mechanized agriculture imposed modern business techniques on Mississippi farmers and contributed to the out-migration of surplus farm labor. Finally, after more than a hundred years, Mississippians freed themselves from the tyranny of King Cotton. In his place came agricultural diversification. Mississippi farmers by 1972 were earning more than twice as much from livestock as from cotton. Receipts from soybeans amounted to 70 percent of the dollars earned from cotton.

In the middle of the 1960s, Mississippi became an industrial state. For the first time in the state's history, jobs in manufacturing outnumbered those in agriculture. A great cheer went up from the politicians. Former Governor Hugh L. White, father of Mississippi's modern drive for industrialization and by then a very old man, was feted and praised. Certainly, the transition was a landmark event, but, one must hasten to add, Mississippi still had not become industrialized in the national sense of that term. Lacking natural resources except water and timber, Mississippi's industrial base relies heavily on garment plants and wood products, two of the lowest-paying industries in the nation. Heavy industry and industries requiring superior technology were still, in the 1970s, largely absent.

Yet seldom do Mississippians complain, for measured against their own background of poverty, the citizens of the state by the 1970s enjoyed relative prosperity. In a statewide poll conducted in 1974, Mississippians almost unanimously believed wages to be better, educational opportunities greater, the state a better place to live, and the general quality of life in Mississippi much improved over that of preceding decades. Unlike many of their fellow Americans who were mired in self-doubt and criticism, Mississippians in the mid-seventies bubbled with confidence. The optimism was not mere boosterism. Between 1948 and 1975, per-capita income in Mississippi rose from $789 to $4,041, from 55 percent of national per-capita income to almost 70 percent. Despite grave problems remaining from the past—a narrow tax base, a tradition of meager social services, and a political leadership that failed to recognize that government must also change as the economic and demographic patterns are altered—Mississippians rediscovered "progress," just as their fellow Americans first began to question it.

One of the myths of our time is that government leads. In fact government usually only adjusts to economic and social changes that have already occurred. In the 1970s, political reality in Mississippi began to follow the industrial and demographic revolutions that had begun in 1945.

One day in the mid-1960s, I picked up my newspaper to see what the legislature was doing. At that time, the lawmakers were engaged in heated debate concerning (1) prohibition, (2) evolution, and (3) the right of women to sit on juries. Suddenly I felt as if I had been transported back into the 1920s. Ten years later, I picked up my newspaper to see Charles Evers, the state's most famous and controversial black civil rights leader and Medgar Evers's brother, and E. L. McDaniel, former Grand Dragon of the United Ku Klux Klan, appearing on the same platform and paying compliments to each other in the best good-ole-boy style. "I count Mayor Evers as a friend now and I have a lot of respect for the man,'' said McDaniel. ''We realized it's not blacks against whites, but the little folks against the big shots,'' said Evers.[11] Their compliments mirrored a dramatic political realignment, a coalition of poor blacks and poor whites dreamed of by populists for decades, but always before unrealized because race overrode class interest.

In 1975 Cliff Finch, lunch box in his hand, hard hat on his head, rode into the governor's mansion seated on a bulldozer, as the ''working man's'' candidate. In 1976 Jimmy Carter became the first Democratic presidential nominee to carry Mississippi since Adlai Stevenson in 1956. Behind both of these phenomena lay a political realignment along economic lines, not race.

Since the Voting Rights Act of 1965, more than 250,000 black Mississippians have been registered to vote. Because of low voter turnouts, they have not often wielded enough power to bring blacks to office even in those counties that are heavily black. But the existence of the black vote provided two subtle changes in Mississippi politics. First, white candidates could not ignore the black vote; race-baiting as a political technique was largely absent from Mississippi elections after 1967. But more important, the absence of the race question in politics allowed Mississippians for the first time in a generation to examine real political issues, and many of these were economic. For the first time in Mississippi history, blacks and whites aligned politically on real issues. The artificial solidarity produced by the race issue is gone.

Cliff Finch was elected governor in 1975 with the support of Klansmen and civil rights leaders. Political columnists from Washington say that the black vote carried Mississippi for Jimmy Carter in 1976. Perhaps so, but Jimmy Carter got his largest majorities in rural white counties where the black vote is negligible. Politics, usually the last institution to change, is finally catching up to Mississippi's altered economic and social systems.

Receding too is the siege mentality of the 1950s and 1960s. In the aftermath of the Meredith crisis of 1962, Ole Miss his-

11. *Hattiesburg American*, May 22, 1977.

tory professor James W. Silver wrote a book entitled *Mississippi: The Closed Society*. Silver had come to the university in the mid-thirties and stayed. Long before 1962, Silver developed a reputation not unusual on university campuses, but rare among politicians and businessmen, for being independent, blunt, outspoken, and irascible. But he found life in Mississippi pleasant and ingratiating if, as he noted, one did not go counter to the racial orthodoxy. In *The Closed Society,* which first appeared in 1963 at the apex of violence, white resistance to civil rights, and extremist intimidation, Silver stated a simple thesis. For a century, he said, Mississippi whites had paid homage to an orthodoxy—a set of beliefs such as white supremacy, the lost-cause myth, and the myths surrounding Reconstruction. Anyone who questioned the orthodoxy or whose conduct went counter to accepted conventions was forced to conform or to leave. The result, according to Silver, was an intellectual wall that sealed off Mississippi. New ideas and able men could leave, but few could enter, producing a talent drain that almost insured that Mississippi's best and brightest would depart. Those who adapted to the orthodoxy stayed, thus insuring its perpetuation. The book created a furor. Many reactions seemed to prove Silver's thesis. Newspapers, politicians, and private citizens called for Silver's removal from the university. Usually, the reasoning went: he is being paid by the people of Mississippi; he should respect and reflect their views; if he cannot, he should resign or be fired.

While Silver's thesis was largely true in Mississippi in 1963–1964, the closed society was not uniformly tightly shut. Openings of tolerance existed in the state even as he wrote the book. Greenville, traditionally a tolerant town and the home of Hodding Carter's *Delta-Democrat Times,* never completely shut out the outside world. Neither did the cosmopolitan Gulf Coast. Academic freedom in the classrooms of the universities and colleges was not everywhere infringed. What Silver could not foresee as he wrote *The Closed Society* was the immediacy of its collapse. Ironically, as Silver wrote, the walls of intellectual isolation he was describing already were undermined and in 1965 would begin to crumble suddenly and completely. Along with King Cotton, mass poverty, sharecropping, and Jim Crowism, Mississippi's stubborn insularity and isolation fell under the onslaught of economic change. Mississippians found that a society may not pick and choose what it wants to accept from another culture. White Mississippians would have superimposed industrialism and affluence over their old unchanged social and political orders. They could not. Mississippians could not keep at bay the values and ideals of the rest of the nation while accepting the economic benefits.

Those who have felt challenged for decades to eradicate Mississippi's peculiarities and to remold Mississippi in the national image may safely rest from their work. The Americanization of Mississippi has been under way since 1945 and for good or bad cannot be reversed. In the past, Mississippians have been able on occasion to turn back the racial clock, but in those instances in 1875 and 1890, they found it possible because nothing had really changed economically. The economic revolution in Mississippi since 1945 has already mandated racial accommodation and demographic change, and, in the future, perhaps governmental change.

Epilogue

THE history of Mississippi is heavy with irony. Mississippians accept the two worlds of illusion and reality as a part of life, but outsiders find her anomalies hard to understand. I remember once attempting to explain Mississippi's Black-Market Tax to a Californian. Mississippi retained statewide prohibition until 1966; but in those areas of the state where public opinion was wet—the Mississippi River counties and the Gulf Coast—liquor was sold openly. So that the state could collect revenue on this illegal commodity, the legislature levied a 10 percent tax on liquor. Mississippi for two decades found herself in the illogical position of taxing an illegal commodity. Outsiders found the arrangement puzzling, but to Mississippians, it made perfect sense—the Baptists had their prohibition law, drinkers had their liquor, and state received the taxes. Everybody was happy.

A love-hate ambivalence pervades the Mississippi character. Mississippians love the land, and they curse it. Even black expatriates who migrated to the ghettos of the North to escape the economic and social oppressions of Jim Crowism feel the tug of home. Before Christmas, package-packed cars with Michigan or Illinois tags fill the highways. Many admit that only jobs and money keep them in the North. In fact, some estimates indicate that, since 1970, Mississippi's black population has started to rise again, the result of returning expatriates. This love-hate relationship has always dominated race relations. When Barnett or Bilbo reminded us that they loved blacks and had many black friends, non-Mississippians snickered, but the two politicians were serious. Their protestations reflected a generations-old relationship—one group dominant and the other subservient. Within that context, genuine affections and friendships were worked out.

In the mid-1970s, an obituary for the race question, the central theme of Mississippi history, might seem premature; yet, for the first time in more than a century, Mississippians seem more interested in economic progress than in race.

Still other ironies stare out from Mississippi's past. A state that consistently ranks near the bottom in education produced some of the greatest writers in American literature. A state that for generations has been known as the most stubborn stronghold of racism is at the same time one of the most democratic—not just political democracy, but genuine egalitarianism. Mississippi seldom had an aristocracy of power or wealth, so poverty perhaps bred democracy.

Many hallmarks of Mississippi history are gone, and few would lament their passing. In the nineteenth century, Mississippians bequeathed to their region and to the nation the First and Second Mississippi plans. Both served as models for Mississippi's sister states of the South. By the beginning of this century, Mississippi held the leadership of reaction in the South. In the first instance in 1875, Mississippi Democrats used violence, intimidation, and fraud to restore the antebellum racial order. Their legacy to later Mississippians was a democracy for whites only and a system for keeping the black man down that was of such supreme importance that to maintain it no price was too high to pay—economic poverty, political fraud, or outright brutality. In 1890 the Second Mississippi Plan proved that democracy could be circumvented by legal chicanery. After the United States Supreme Court found nothing unconstitutional in Mississippi's discriminatory voting provisions in the Constitution of 1890, virtually every other former Confederate state enacted similar plans. Surely the most nostalgic Mississippian would not lament the passing of Jim Crow and sharecropping. No more must Mississippians feel isolated and defensive. No longer must they defend a peculiar society to other Americans. The 1960s proved to all Americans that the oppression of blacks was not peculiar to Mississippi or even to the American South.

Another of Mississippi's gloomy legacies is poverty. As many historians have noted about the South, it is the only section to know poverty in a nation of plenty. That statement applies doubly for Mississippi. How much Mississippi's traditional agrarian poverty in an industrial nation encouraged other dark factors in the state's history is entirely a subjective judgment. Yet one must suspect that poverty spurred a feeling of persecution, violence, isolation, a paucity of political leadership, and historical myth-making. For more than a century, the economic fortunes of Mississippians were tied to King Cotton. In good years, when prices were high, cotton seemed like magic. In bad years, it brought ruin. Mississippians cannot regret being freed from the vagaries of that one-crop economy and the general poverty that it produced for all but a few. Certainly few Mississippians would revive that feudal order.

Geography, so important in producing sectionalism, no longer plays a great role in fashioning affairs. Mississippians, like most other Americans, find themselves increasingly homogenized. Seldom does one hear the hill farmers of the east sneeringly damn the Delta planters or the Delta planters insultingly mutter "Redneck" in reply.

If these Mississippi hallmarks are gone, others are worth retaining. The egalitarianism and familiarity of the frontier, if extended to blacks, is worth cherishing in a nation increasingly unequal and divided. The fierce individualism, so often characteristic of the state, with its defensiveness and sense of persecution removed, is worth preserving. The pull of home and ties to the soil in a nation where rootlessness has been raised to a virtue is refreshing. The pride, less the stubbornness, can produce unity.

One views the passing of the old order with some ambivalence, for as morally and economically cramping as it was, it had a certain familiarity and uniqueness. One fears that the Americanization of Mississippi, although inevitable, will make Mississippi like Iowa, or Indiana, or some other state; and such loss of identity would be sad. Mississippians may soon realize that "progress" has her cost: pollution, crowded highways, loss of individual identity, Yankee organization and efficiency. Sometimes the nasal, clipped twang of Yankee voices in supermarkets must evoke a longing for the old insularity.

As one leaves the mouth of the Pascagoula River, he sees looming to his left the biggest industry in Mississippi, Ingalls Shipyard, employing twenty thousand workers. Farther down the beach, one sees a Standard Oil refinery and a chemical plant at Bayou Casotte. It is then that the Mississippian must long for the days when the coast was dotted only by a chain of fishing villages. But in those days he could not have bought his boat.

Mississippi has not attained perfection. Problems persist. Mississippi is still the poorest state in the nation, by most standards. Thus the tax base is narrow and government services primitive. Government has not yet caught up with the vast changes of the last generation in economics and population. The quality of Mississippi's labor force will not support many sophisticated, high-wage industries. But these are problems of the mind, not problems of the spirit. Mississippi has hurdled the latter. Among Mississippians today, an optimism flourishes about the nation and its future, maybe because Mississippians are just now beginning to enjoy the fruits of American life, while other Americans already are jaded.

What of Mississippi's future? One would like to predict that Mississippi will retain the best of the old and receive what is good from the new, that she can have the affluence of industrialization without the pollution and problems, that she can have the fruits of urbanization without crime and crowding. Mississippians at the nation's bicentennial were winning their old battles with themselves—poverty, race, insularity, and persecution. Now they face a new challenge: how to become Americans without ceasing to be Mississippians.

Suggestions for Further Reading

Several general histories of Mississippi exist today. The best and most complete is *A History of Mississippi,* edited by Richard A. McLemore, 2 volumes (Hattiesburg: University and College Press of Mississippi, 1973). Financially sponsored by the state of Mississippi, the three state universities, and the Mississippi Historical Society, this two-volume work contains forty-three chapters written by forty-one authors. An older and less useful general history is Dunbar Rowland's *Mississippi: Heart of the South,* 2 volumes (Chicago: S. J. Clarke Publishing Company, 1925). Still older is J. F. H. Claiborne's *Mississippi as a Province, Territory, and State* (Jackson: Power and Barksdale, Publishers and Printers, 1880). This work was the first volume of a projected two-volume history. The second volume was never published. Volume I, which ends with statehood, was reprinted in 1964 by Louisiana State University Press. Two texts are John K. Bettersworth's *Your Mississippi* (Austin: Steck-Vaughn Company, 1975) and *Mississippi: Conflict and Change* (New York: Pantheon Books, 1974), edited by Charles Sallis and James L. Loewen. Two periodical sources are of great value in the study of Mississippi history. *The Journal of Mississippi History* has been in continuous quarterly publication since 1939 and contains articles on various topics in Mississippi history. *The Publications of the Mississippi Historical Society* is the older publication of that organization, published from 1898 to 1925.

Excellent accounts of early explorers in Mississippi are contained in *Spanish Explorers in the Southern United States* (New York: Barnes and Noble, Inc., 1946). For that volume, Theodore H. Lewis edited the journal of de Soto's expedition, "The Narrative of Hernando de Soto By the Gentleman of Elvas." It is a fascinating first-hand account of de Soto's travels. In the same volume is the similar "Narrative of Álvar Núñez Cabeza de Vaca" edited by Frederick W. Hodge. Fascinating journals of the French explorers Marquette, La Salle, and Tonty are contained in *Early Narratives of the Northwest, 1634–1699* edited by Louise Phelps Kellogg (New York: Charles Scribner's Sons, 1917) and *The Journeys of Rene Robert Cavelier Sieur de La Salle,* edited by Isaac Joslin Cox, 2 volumes (New York: Alberton Book Company, 1908).

For the founding of French Louisiana, see Nellis M. Crouse, *Lemoyne d'Iberville, Soldier of New France* (Ithaca: Cornell University Press, 1954) and Iberville's narrative of his expedition contained in B. F. French, *Historical Collections of Louisiana* (New York: Wiley and Putnam, 1846). No complete history of the Louisiana colony exists in the English language. Very useful for official correspondence between French Louisiana and Paris is *Mississippi Provincial Archives: French Dominion,* edited by Dunbar Rowland and Albert G. Sanders, 3 volumes (Jackson: Press of the Mississippi Department of Archives and History, 1927).

Two general studies cover British West Florida. The most complete is Cecil Johnson's *British West Florida, 1763–1783* (New Haven: Yale University Press, 1943). Less complete is *The British Development of West Florida, 1763–1769* by Clinton Howard (Berkeley: University of California Press, 1947). Dunbar Rowland's *Mississippi Provincial Archives: The English Dominion* (Nashville: Press of Brandon Printing Company, 1911) contains official correspondence between British officials in West Florida and the Board of Trade in London. The effect of the American Revolution on the Natchez area is told in Robert Haynes, *The Natchez District and the American Revolution* (Jackson: The University Press of Mississippi, 1976).

One may gain a good understanding of the Spanish period in Mississippi history by reading two books: Arthur P. Whitaker's *The Spanish-American Frontier: 1783–1795, The Westward Movement and the Spanish Retreat in the Mississippi Valley* (New York: Houghton Mifflin Company, 1927) and Jack D. L. Holmes's *Gayoso: The Life of a Spanish Governor in the Mississippi Valley, 1789–1799* (Baton Rouge:

Louisiana State University Press, 1965). The latter volume is more than a simple biography, for it also contains the best economic, political, and social description yet published of the Natchez District under Spanish rule.

No complete history of the territorial period has been published, but a number of excellent studies cover the period from statehood to the Civil War. Charles S. Sydnor wrote two books about antebellum Mississippi that have become classics. They are *Slavery in Mississippi* (New York: D. Appleton-Century Company, 1933) and the biographical *A Gentleman of the Old Natchez Region: Benjamin L. C. Wailes* (Durham: Duke University Press, 1938). D. Clayton James's *Antebellum Natchez* (Baton Rouge: Louisiana State University Press, 1968) is an excellent and readable survey of the Natchez area from French settlement to the Civil War. A political study covering the 1820s and 1830s is *Jacksonian Democracy in Mississippi,* by Edwin A. Miles (Chapel Hill: University of North Carolina Press, 1960). The story of Indian removal is told in Arthur H. DeRosier, *The Removal of the Choctaw Indians* (Knoxville: The University of Tennessee Press, 1970). The highly entertaining and humorous *The Flush Times of Alabama and Mississippi,* by Joseph G. Baldwin (New York: D. Appleton and Company, 1853), gives the flavor of the freewheeling frontier in Mississippi of the 1830s and 1840s. The title of John H. Moore's *Agriculture in Antebellum Mississippi* (New York: Bookman Associates, 1958) is self-explanatory. The best study of secession in Mississippi is *Mississippi: Storm Center of Secession, 1856–1861,* by Percy L. Rainwater (Baton Rouge: Otto Claitor, 1938).

For the Civil War, there is no really excellent military history of the war in Mississippi. *Decision in Mississippi,* by Edwin Bearss (Jackson: Commission on the War Between the States, 1962) covers the subject, but it is highly disorganized and haphazardly written. Volume II of Shelby Foote's *The Civil War* (New York: Random House, 1963) contains an excellent book-length treatment of the Vicksburg campaign. *Grierson's Raid,* by D. Alexander Brown (Urbana: University of Illinois Press, 1954), is the story of one of the most daring and effective cavalry raids of the entire war. Two good accounts of the nonmilitary aspects of the war in Mississippi are John K. Bettersworth's *Confederate Mississippi: The People and Politics of a Cotton State in Wartime* (Baton Rouge: Louisiana State University Press,

1943) and Peter F. Walker's *Vicksburg: A People at War, 1860–1865* (Chapel Hill: University of North Carolina Press, 1960).

For Reconstruction, see the old but still very useful *Reconstruction in Mississippi,* by James W. Garner (New York: The Macmillan Company, 1901). Garner paints the old traditional view of Reconstruction in Mississippi. A newer, revisionist view is William C. Harris's *Presidential Reconstruction in Mississippi* (Baton Rouge: Louisiana State University Press, 1967), which covers the period from 1865 to 1867. Forthcoming is *Congressional Reconstruction in Mississippi* by the same author.

Two classic state studies cover the late nineteenth and early twentieth centuries. Vernon L. Wharton's *The Negro in Mississippi, 1865–1890* (Chapel Hill: University of North Carolina Press, 1947), is outstanding. The political history of the state after Reconstruction is contained in *Revolt of the Rednecks 1876–1925* by Albert D. Kirwan (Lexington: University of Kentucky Press, 1951).

For Mississippi history since 1925, hardly any historical scholarship exists. Only the modern civil-rights movement has produced significant historical literature. In that area, the best works are James W. Silver, *Mississippi: The Closed Society* (New York: Harcourt, Brace, and World, Inc., 1963); Russell H. Barrett, *Integration at Ole Miss* (Chicago: Quadrangle Books, 1965); and Walter Lord, *The Past That Would Not Die* (London: Hamish Hamilton, 1966). Two books containing material on the rise and role of Mississippi Citizens' Councils are Hodding Carter III, *The South Strikes Back* (Garden City, New York: Doubleday, 1959) and Neil R. McMillen, *The Citizens' Councils: Organized Resistance to the Second Reconstruction, 1954–1964* (Urbana: University of Illinois Press, 1971).

Literary criticism of Mississippi authors is incredibly voluminous. One of the best assessments of Faulkner's work is Cleanth Brooks, *William Faulkner: The Yoknapatawpha Country* (New Haven: Yale University Press, 1963). For enlightening information on both Faulkner's and Welty's writings, see Louis D.Rubin, *The Faraway Country: Writers of the Modern South* (Seattle: University of Washington Press, 1963). *Novelists' America: Fiction as History, 1910–1940,* by Nelson Manfred Blake (Syracuse: Syracuse University Press, 1969), contains excellent chapters on William Faulkner and Richard Wright and the historical roots of their fiction.

No single volume outlines the development of blues music in Mississippi, but Paul Oliver's *The Story of the Blues* (New York: Chilton Book Company, 1969) contains much interesting information on the origins of the blues and the central role played by Mississippi blues musicians. *Blow My Blues Away,* by George Mitchell (Baton Rouge: Louisiana State University Press, 1971), has interviews and impressions of many Mississippi blues singers who were still alive in the late 1960s.

Reminiscences, biographies, and autobiographies are too numerous to list. Reminiscences were popular in nineteenth-century Mississippi, and two of the best are W. H. Sparks, *The Memories of Fifty Years* (Philadelphia: Claxton, Remsen, and Haffelfinger, 1870) and Reuben Davis, *Recollections of Mississippi and Mississippians,* first published in 1889 but recently reprinted (Hattiesburg: The University and College Press of Mississippi, 1972). *The Barber of Natchez,* by Edwin A. Davis and William R. Hogan (Baton Rouge: Louisiana State University Press, 1954), is the fascinating biography of a free Negro who rose to wealth and prominence in antebellum Natchez. There are many biographies of Jefferson Davis. One of the best is *Jefferson Davis: The Unreal and the Real,* by Robert McElroy, 2 volumes (New York: Harper and Brothers, 1937). Biographies of two great protagonists of Reconstruction are Lillian A. Pereyra, *James Lusk Alcorn: Persistent Whig* (Baton Rouge: Louisiana State University Press, 1966) and *Adelbert Ames, 1835–1933,* by Blanche Ames (New York: Argosy-Antiquarian, Ltd., 1964). William F. Holmes has written the definitive biography of Mississippi's most important twentieth-century politician, *The White Chief, James Kimble Vardaman* (Baton Rouge: Louisiana State University Press, 1970). The only biography of his political descendant is *The Man Bilbo* by A. Wigfall Green (Baton Rouge: Louisiana State University Press, 1963). It is short, sketchy, and shallow. The definitive biography of Bilbo has not yet been written. Two excellent autobiographies both deal with the twentieth century. William Alexander Percy's *Lanterns on the Levee: Recollections of a Planter's Son* (New York: A. A. Knopf, 1941) is one of the best autobiographies ever written by a Southerner. Anne Moody's *Coming of Age in Mississippi* (New York: The Dial Press, Inc., 1968) is the best autobiographical book to come out of the civil-rights movement in Mississippi.

Index